PELON

The Untold Story of a Yuma Hero

J. Hernandez

Copyright © 2024 by J. Hernandez

All rights reserved. No part of this book may be reproduced or transmitted in any form or by any means, electronic or mechanical, including photocopying, recording, or by any information storage and retrieval system, without permission in writing from the author.

Published by: **JaimeBondo.com**

Rob Bignell
Editor

Erickson Ludewig
Illustrator

While some characters, events, and locations are inspired by real people and historical events, the story and its characters are largely the product of the author's imagination.

Library of Congress Control Number: 2025904542

ISBN: 979-8-9926822-2-9

Dedication

This book is dedicated to my Mariolas

I extend my heartfelt gratitude for your unwavering support. My exploration of Yuma's history commenced in the 1990s during my tenure at the Yuma Territorial Prison State Historic Park. I would like to express my profound appreciation to my former supervisor, Jesse Torres, whose dedication to our history and heritage has left a lasting impact.

Introduction

In January 2024, I embarked on a research journey at the Yuma County Library to gather material for this book. The library houses an extensive collection of local literature and newspapers in microfilm. Accompanied by my dedicated team of researchers, who happen to be my kids but are nonetheless highly efficient, our objective was to uncover and document the legends of Yuma. We found unacknowledged beauty and pride in this region. This book presents historically accurate accounts from the desert Southwest.

Pelon, a figure shrouded in both legend and fact, is crucial to understanding the turbulent history of the desert Southwest. We possess only fragmented glimpses of his life, marked by extraordinary events reflecting the region's harsh and often lawless nature. Through his endeavors, Pelon emerged as a symbol of resilience and tenacity, navigating the challenging landscapes and fierce conflicts of his time. His determination mirrors that of his people, the great Quechan.

The objective of this book is to vividly depict Pelon through these narratives. History often provides only a monochrome outline of past events; I have endeavored to add color to them. The events described span from approximately 1847 to 1890, capturing the essence of a period when the rugged and untamed landscape of the southwest was influenced by its inhabitants' ambitions, struggles, and triumphs.

Through meticulous research and a dedication to uncovering the past, this book delves into the stories of individuals like Paddy Burke, whose lives and actions have significantly shaped the history and heritage of Yuma and the broader region. This work aims to celebrate and preserve the legacy of those who forged their paths in the captivating and challenging desert Southwest.

Join me on this journey through time as we explore tales of resilience, bravery, and spirit that define the legends of Yuma.

Paddy Meets Pelon

At that time, Yuma was known as Colorado City. Paddy was very familiar with the town, as he had been stationed across the river at Fort Yuma. During his visit, Paddy stopped by his old Fort, and there, he purchased provisions from the quartermaster's depot. While at the depot, he saw four soldiers mocking a young Indigenous man, kicking and tripping him for amusement. Disturbed by this, Paddy approached the soldiers, who recognized him as Officer Burke despite his current civilian status. They saluted him with a resounding "Sir!" and squared their positions.

Paddy stoically returned the salute and questioned them, "Has this young lad been sentenced to humiliation?"

The soldiers exchanged puzzled looks.

When they didn't respond, he pressed further, asking, "Very well, what is the sentence this young on' carries, then?"

One soldier finally responded hesitantly, "Th-this prisoner is a danger to the other Indians, s-Sir."

Paddy replied, "Is that so? Then I shall speak with the Quartermaster General. As logic serves, this frail young lad, truly a danger to his community, then he should answer to Indian law. If he be a danger to the territory, he would answer to the Sheriff. Similarly, if he be considered a danger to the United States, he would answer to the U.S. Army."

The young man had grown up cautious of white men. All the tales from the elders speak of caution and distrust toward this particular neighbor. Because he understood the tongue of the white men, Pelon was amazed by the old soldier's kindness and cunning. He saw how he talked his way out of the shackles that bound him, and how he faced the Quartermaster General with courage and respect. He was confused yet relieved that he had met a white man that was not interested in his demise. He felt gratitude and admiration for the old soldier, who had a name that sounded like Burke.

Pelon was now free to go back to his people, but he felt a strange pull toward Paddy. He scattered as soon as he was let out of his shackles and found a good hiding place. He wondered what kind of man Paddy was, and what he was doing in this land. He decided to hide in the livery and follow him the next day and see where he went. Paddy had a fine horse and a team of mules. He took Paddy's horse and saddle and began to care for them. He brushed the horse, cleaned the hooves,

and oiled the saddle with neatsfoot oil. By the time Paddy was ready to leave, the boy had finished and done very well at that.

Paddy arrived at the livery and as he prepared to leave, approached Pelon silently. Pelon had shown Paddy that he was grateful and that he had skills.

Paddy saw the boy and smiled. "Laddie, ye have character, coming back to repay me with the sweat of yer braw. I like that, I do. Good lad. Ye have a name, lad?"

Pelon nodded and said his name.

Paddy repeated it, and said, "Well, Pelon, ye have done a fine job with me horse and saddle. Here, take this." He tossed a silver piece to Pelon, who caught it with ease. "Son, I'll be back in a month's due time, and me horse will need yer good care again. Will ye do that for me?"

Pelon nodded again.

"Good lad!" said Paddy and mounted his horse. He waved to Pelon and rode away.

Pelon waited for a month for Paddy to return. He would head back to the livery at night, taking care of the horses and learning from the owner, Paco. Paco was a kind man who treated Pelon with respect and allowed him to stay in the stables. He also taught him how to ride, harness, and trim hooves. Pelon was fascinated by the different breeds and colors of the horses, and he soon learned their names and personalities.

Pelon had a special bond with one horse, a chestnut mare named Ruby. She was gentle and intelligent, and she seemed to understand Pelon's words and gestures. She would nuzzle his hand, follow his commands, and let him ride her without a saddle or bridle. Pelon loved Ruby, and he hoped that he would be able to buy her someday.

Pelon also made friends with some of the other boys who worked at the livery. They were two Mexican kids and one Indian, like him, and they shared stories and jokes mostly in Spanish. They also played games of marbles, sticks, or raced their horses around the town. Paco didn't like it when they raced the horses, and they would get in trouble. Pelon felt happy and free in Colorado City, unlike in the mission or on the reservation.

One day, as Pelon was grooming Ruby, he heard a familiar voice. He looked up and saw Paddy walking toward him, smiling broadly. He was accompanied by two other men, one white and one black, who carried bags and tools. They looked tired but satisfied, as if they had just completed a successful journey.

"Hello, lad! Ya' still here!" Paddy exclaimed, clapping Pelon on the shoulder. "I'm glad to see ya'. How've you been?"

Pelon grinned and nodded, unable to speak. He was overjoyed to see Paddy Burke. "I've been well, sir. And you?" he managed to say.

"Oh, I've been fine, fine. We've just come back from Fort Tyson (later known as Quartzsite), looked at a claim for Hank here. It turned out to be a rich vein of silver, worth a fortune. We helped him stake it and value it, and we'll get a share of the profits. Isn't that right, boys?" He turned to his companions.

"That's right, Paddy. You did a fine job, as always. We owe you a lot," the white man said. He had blond hair, blue eyes, and a bushy red beard. He wore a wide-brimmed Mexican hat and a leather jacket. He introduced himself as Hank, the owner of the Home Ticket claim.

"How ya' doin' Pelon? Paddy done told us all 'bout ya'," the black man said. He had dark skin, brown eyes, and a shaved head. He wore a checkered shirt, denim pants, and a bandana. He introduced himself as Sam. Pelon hadn't seen many black men before. Paddy later explained Sam was a former slave who had escaped to the West and became a prospector and a friend.

Pelon nodded and shook hands with both men, feeling shy but proud. He was amazed by their stories and accomplishments. He had never met anyone like them before.

"Come on, lad. Let's take care of me horse. She must be tired after the long trip," Burke said, leading Pelon to the stable.

"Take our horses, too, young man," said Hank. "You can tell me all about what you've been doing here. And tomorrow, we'll have a feast and a celebration. You're part of the team now, Pelon. You're one of us."

The Glanton Gang

The following day, Paddy and his team enjoyed a feast at Schoenberger's place before heading out to meet two of Paddy's friends, Heepah and Schem, who were Yuma Indians. The name Yuma was given by the Spanish explorers to the Kwatsaan or Quechan people, who were Paddy's trusted allies. They needed to cross the river, so Paddy and Pelon proceeded to the ferry.

Pelon suggested, "Maybe we should wait for the Indian ferry."

"Nonsense!" retorted Paddy.

As they approached, Paddy reminisced about former ferry operators, John Joel Glanton and his goons. He had crossed paths with the infamous gun slinger and he told Pelon about it.

Some eight years before, Paddy had left the enlisted ranks of the army, moved to Tucson and was back in Yuma for some business along with a Yuma Indian acquaintance. Upon their arrival, Glanton, a dishonored soldier with a tarnished reputation, recognized Paddy. He greeted him with a formal "Sir!" to which Paddy replied, "Pleasant morning."

After this exchange, Glanton turned to Paddy's companion and scolded him, "Boy! What are you doing pestering this gentleman? I've told you not to go near the river again! Leave and don't come back!" Then turning to Paddy, Glanton added, "I apologize, sir, these varmints need to be treated accordingly, or they will be bothersome. And they have their own ferry, not to be bothering a fine gentleman as yourself. They're like dogs, I tell ya.'"

Paddy then stepped forward, lifted his chin, looked Glanton in the eye, and firmly stated, "This lad is with me, and you'll treat him as me kin."

Glanton nervously laughed and briefly weighed his options; though he had three men on his side, he knew Paddy Burke's tough nature and grit. For a moment, time seemed to halt, and even the river appeared to pause in anticipation of Glanton's next move. Glanton was not accustomed to being spoken to in such a manner and letting it slide. In the past, he'd shot a man for merely bumping into him without remorse. But something inside him made him reconsider the confrontation, and he responded meekly, "Sir!" The formidable Glanton had been intimidated by Paddy.

Pelon felt proud and grateful but hid his emotions and continued to listen intently to the story. He couldn't ignore that Paddy not only defended the Indian friend from Glanton but also considered him family. He wondered why Paddy held such authority over the bully.

As Paddy was telling his story, the ferry made its way to their side of the river. The operator promptly invited them to board the ferry and cross the river. He guided Paddy's horse, along with a pair of mules and milking goats, toward the ferry. He charged a dollar each, which Paddy paid unhesitatingly. Pelon mounted one of the mules while Paddy got on his own horse. They followed the operator to the ferry, which was a wooden raft pulled across the water by ropes. During the crossing, Paddy continued with his Glanton experience. And as they made their way across the river, Paddy confided to Pelon that he had known about Glanton for a long time and had waited for an opportunity to kill him.

Paddy explained a dark shadow that loomed over the region. Paddy's story was that Glanton, a ruthless scalper and leader of a gang of scalp hunters, had been terrorizing tribes all over the New Mexico Territory for years. Glanton's exploits took place through the 1840s, a time of great turmoil and violence in the territory.

Glanton joined the regulars for the army in the past. He felt the uniform gave him a license to kill at free will. But the army would not have it and he was jailed and consequently received a dishonorable discharge. In Paddy's account, Glanton should have been executed by a firing squad, but his commander went soft on him. He had developed a hatred for Mexicans and Indians, whom he considered inferior and savage. He had also become addicted to alcohol and gambling, which fueled his violent impulses. He had gathered a band of misfits and outlaws, mostly army deserters from the war, who shared his lust for blood and money.

The Glanton gang later operated in the area around the Colorado River, which formed the border between California and the New Mexico territory. They would often cross into the New Mexico territory to hunt and scalp Native Americans, taking advantage of the political instability and lack of effective law enforcement in the region. The Glanton gang's involvement in scalping was a brutal and lucrative business, carried out first under the guise of a government-sponsored program and for their personal enjoyment afterwards.

Paddy was made aware of less known business of trade in human hair, particularly the long hair of Indian women, which was highly prized for its beauty and length. Glanton and his gang became involved in this trade, forcibly taking Indian women and children captive, and cutting off their hair.

The hair business was a thriving trade at the time, with the hair being sold to wig makers and hair merchants in the United States and Europe. Glanton and his gang saw an opportunity to profit from this trade and they systematically hunted down and captured Yuma Indian women and children, cutting off their hair and selling it to the highest bidder. This practice was not only incredibly cruel but also deeply traumatic for the Yuma people, who, at the same time, were facing violence, displacement, and marginalization. The hair business perpetuated a culture of violence and exploitation that started with scalping, and Glanton's involvement in it is a stark reminder of the brutal treatment of Native American tribes during this period.

Pelon listened intently and thought, "these are the bad men our elders teach us about..."

After a wave of Americans went across, led by Major Anderson, it was a wave of Mexicans coming across the Colorado. This caused the Glanton gang to become envious of the non-American ferry's increased business. The gang kidnapped a Yuma chief along with the ferry operator, but they released the chief days later. They did, however, murder the operator, who was a former U.S. soldier.

Glanton got greedy and was soon killing Opatas, Pimas and Mexicans for their scalps. This was discovered by the authorities who then put a bounty on his gang. His reign of terror eventually came to an end in 1851, when Glanton and his gang were ambushed and killed by a group of Yuma Indians and Mexican soldiers. The same chief who escaped the earlier kidnapping had planned a revenge. He took action once the Glantons returned from a San Diego trip. Upon his return, the gang celebrated and drank their spirits. The chief made his way to the place of celebration and joined. His men were placed on both sides of the river. With a wave of a handkerchief, the chief ordered the attack, and the gang was slaughtered. Paddy told this story with hints of regret for not having killed Glanton himself.

Paddy then pivoted to Heepah and Schem. He had known the two Yumas for a long time. They are mother and daughter, and they are healers. They had met after the Mexican War and during the conflict between the Yuma tribe and the U.S. Army that lasted to 1853. Paddy had been a soldier then, fighting against the Yumas. But he had grown disillusioned with the war and eventually mustered out to Tucson. While in Yuma, he had wandered into the desert, where he encountered Heepah and Schem. They took him in as family and showed him life outside the village. He would spend more time with them than with his regiment. Paddy had learned their language and culture and had become close friends.

Paddy said it was his intention for Pelon to learn from Heepah and Schem and let them guide Pelon in ways of the spirit. Paddy said that he visited them often, and that they always welcomed him as family. He said that he would introduce Pelon to them, and that they would help him learn more about the desert and its secrets.

They reached the other side of the river and disembarked from the ferry. They thanked the operator and rode away from the riverbank. Paddy led Pelon to a trail that ran parallel to the river, heading north. He said that Heepah and Schem's farm was about ten miles away, and that they would be there in less than two hours. He said that they should hurry, because he had brought them a feast of roast lamb and bread, and he didn't want to keep them waiting. He said that he hoped Pelon was hungry. Pelon smiled and nodded, feeling excited and curious. He followed Paddy, eager to meet the two Yuma Indians.

More About Paddy

William H. Burke, Esq., affectionately known as Paddy, was a gentleman of significant repute. Paddy was an early pioneer of the Pacific Coast, arriving in California from Boston in 1817. His entrepreneurial endeavors included investments in various Arizona mines, and his real estate holdings in Tucson showcased his astute business acumen. A lasting reminder of his courageous service as a regular in the U.S. Army during the Mexican War was the pronounced limp he carried, result of a bullet wound suffered in action.

Before meeting Pelon, Paddy's most notable accomplishment occurred in 1855, when he performed an audacious patriotic act by raising the first U.S. flag in Arizona — a feat that would become a legend locally. When recounting the event, Paddy would render a dramatic account of how a squad of Mexican soldiers, about to leave Tucson, discovered the citizens' plan to hoist the U.S. flag at the alcalde's office. The Mexican commander, infuriated by what he saw as an insult, confronted the crowd, which greatly outnumbered his men. He demanded the removal of the flag until his squad left town, but the citizens resolutely refused to comply.

The commander, his pride injured, departed in great anger, and the assembled crowd celebrated exuberantly, heralding the occasion as a victory of indomitable will.

Paddy visited Yuma in early 1858 on his way to evaluate the Home Ticket claim in Fort Tyson. Paddy had a keen eye for gold. He had learned the art of prospecting in California. He had joined thousands of other fortune seekers in the foothills of the Sierra Nevada, where he had staked his claims, dug his pits, and panned his dirt. He had also learned how to do proper assessments of a claim's value.

With this knowledge, Paddy had also profited from buying and selling claims. He had a nose for potential and a persuasive tongue for negotiation. He had bought low and sold high, making a handsome profit from his transactions. He had also avoided the pitfalls of fraud, violence, and litigation that plagued many miners. He had earned a reputation as an honest and shrewd businessman, respected by his peers and sought out to perform assessments all over the territory.

Paddy had amassed a considerable fortune from his years in California, but he was not content to rest on his laurels. And he was a man of service, enlisting in the army regulars for the Mexican-American War. He had heard of new discoveries in the New Mexico territory, where the land was rich with silver and copper as well as gold. He had decided to venture into this uncharted territory after his service, seeking new challenges and opportunities. He had packed his wagon with his assaying equipment, his mining tools, and his personal belongings, and headed east. He had crossed the desert, the mountains and valleys, until he reached Tucson.

Spirit Healers

Little is known about the history of Yuma healers, but Paddy was fortunate to have heard these stories. The Yuma healers practice their ancient art of communicating with the spirit world and curing human ailments. But their power comes at a price, as they faced suspicion, hostility, and violence from their own people and the outsiders who invaded their land. Paddy remembers stories that explore the history and culture of the Yuma healers, their struggles and triumphs, their joys and sorrows, and their legacy and fate. These stories are based on historical events and oral traditions, at least what was shared by Heepah and Schem. They were also cautious of other accounts that people might repeat, particularly those that propose that these powers come from above. Heepah would often say these are new accounts, influenced by European contact and that it has led many people to diminish and forget the power that is around them.

According to the healers, in the desolate Box Canyon, located in the vicinity of the Castle Dome Mountains, there is a spring. When a seeker of knowledge approached the spring, a guardian spirit would rise from its depths and ask for his name. The seeker would say his name, and his heart would be measured for goodness. If the seeker is found to be of a bad heart, the guardian and the well would disappear, and the person would find himself stricken by pestilence and die. If the seeker is found to be of good heart, the spring would remain until he drinks from it, and to him was given the power of communicating with the spirit and of healing human disease. The seeker also became a custodian of traditional knowledge.

One of the seekers who found the spring was a young boy named Ahote. He had run away from his tribe after being accused of stealing a horse. He wandered in the desert for days, hungry and thirsty, until he came across the spring. He did not know of its legend, but he felt an overwhelming attraction to the water. He knelt and scooped up some water in his hands. As he brought it to his mouth, he saw a shimmering figure emerge from the spring. It was the guardian spirit, who looked like an old aboriginal man with body and hair covered with white ochre.

"Who are you?" the spirit asked in a deep voice that echoed in the canyon.

"I am Ahote, son of the Desert People," the boy answered, trembling with fear and awe.

The spirit looked at him with piercing eyes. He saw the boy's innocence and courage, his suffering and loneliness. Ahote told him his name and his story, not hiding anything. The spirit nodded and said, "You have been wronged, but you have also done wrong. You have a good heart, but you need guidance. You have found the spring of wisdom, Ahote. You will be able to see the spirits of the land and the people, and you will be able to heal them or harm them. But you will also suffer their pain and their anger. You will be a healer, but you will also be an outcast. Do you accept this fate?"

Ahote hesitated first, but he was desperate and curious. He accepted and drank from the water and felt a surge of energy and vision. He saw the spirit world overlaid on the physical world, and he saw the guardian spirit smiling at him. He thanked him and asked him what he should do next. The spirit told him to go back to his tribe and seek forgiveness and reconciliation. He also told him to find a mentor among the medicine men, one who would teach him the ways of herbs and chanting. He warned him that many would fear him and envy him, and that he would face many trials and temptations.

He told him to always remember his purpose and his duty, and to honor the spirits and the ancestors.

Ahote followed the spirit's advice and returned to his tribe. He confessed he had taken a horse but that it was only to save it from abuse and offered to pay for it. He was forgiven by the chief and the owner of the horse, who were impressed by his honesty and humility. He sought out the oldest and wisest medicine man, who agreed to take him as his apprentice. He learned the secrets of herbs, stones, songs, and prayers. He became a skilled and respected healer who could cure diseases, wounds, and curses. And, as the spirit had warned, he was feared by some but loved by many.

Ahote was known for his extraordinary abilities to heal physical and spiritual ailments using traditional knowledge. He was said to possess a deep understanding of the natural world, allowing him to harness the power of plants, rituals, and spiritual practices to restore balance and harmony.

One notable story about Ahote tells of his encounter with a young girl afflicted by a mysterious illness. She had been brought from a different tribe, where their own medicine men had failed. Ahote spent hours in meditation, seeking guidance from the spirit. He then gathered specific plants and performed a ritual that led to the girl's miraculous recovery.

Ahote's legacy extended beyond his healing abilities. He played a crucial role in preserving the desert people's cultural traditions, stories, and spiritual practices. He never forgot the spring and the guardian spirit, and he visited them often to pay his respects and ask for guidance. His wisdom and teachings continue to inspire and guide his community to this day.

There have been a few who have visited this water and became renowned medicine men. Ernesto was a Cocopah medicine man during the late 1800s. He would be sent to those who had fallen ill. Ernesto would listen to the symptoms and then begin humming his chants. It was described as mummery, as Ernesto entered into a trance and two accompanying men hold him firm to prevent the spirit from carrying him away. Upon awakening, Ernesto seemed fatigued, yet he commenced a more pronounced chanting. This chanting was accompanied by a rattle, and his hands began to wave over the patient. He kept this form for hours and without cessation until the patient improved or died. Ernesto was very successful and had gained a great reputation.

Ernesto also helped find lost or stolen articles. He'd go into a trance, and when he awoke, he'd tell what was communicated by the spirit. He would name the thief and reveal where the item was being kept. Many successful cases have given his clairvoyance great prestige.

La Grippe reached the Cocopah Nation, and 34 people were reported to have died as a consequence. Ernesto was called to help battle this disease, and he performed his rituals. Late that winter, he saw more than 100 people, but still 27 of his patients died. He attended to the Cocopah living in the rancherias along the river. At the same time, the people living in camps away from the river had only seven casualties. When a Cocopah died, it was customary for their relatives to burn their bodies, clothing, food, horses, and cattle. They burned all that the deceased possessed and left their families in perfect destitute.

A group of dissatisfied folks, including Dougherty, Frank, Antonio and others heard rumors that were unfriendly to Ernesto. The rumors implicated Ernesto in the death of the 27 people, and that it was a plot of his and his own family to gain advantage from the death of several heads of family. Dougherty and his gang quickly moved to hunt down and kill Ernesto and his two assistants.

The murders were carried out, and the murderers returned to Yuma assuming they would be safe from prosecution. After all, they had rid the public of three witches. Friends of the murdered men reported the matter to General Torres, Governor of Baja California. The men had traveled to Mexico after the murders and the Governor had them arrested. The Governor was first convinced on imparting justice in this matter. After further deliberation, the Governor decided that the issue should be handled by the United States and that under the existing laws the accused murderers could be taken across the border for trial. He then called on Jose Nar-witch, then General of the Cocopah, and U.S. Colonel D. K. Allen, to handle the situation. General Nar-witch, Colonel Allen, along with Mr. Edward Andrade, took the men into custody and transported them to Los Angeles for arraignment.

Heepah and Schem were Yuma medicine women. They had too gained the power to talk with the spirit and practiced healing. They would be called from every rancheria to attend to ailing women and children. Heepah preferred to be walked by the arm, though her step was sure, she would mostly keep her eyes closed. *"Kawitx ma'a,"* she would often say, asking for a visual impression. Her eyesight was fine, but her preference was to look with her mind's eye. Paddy got a glimpse into her eyes when he first met her. Heepah grabbed both of his hands and looked deep into his eyes and asked, *"Nyanyech ma'a achik,"* which is understood to mean "how are you, my child." Heepah loved Paddy from the first time they met, and he brings a smile to her face in every visit.

When the healers were called to a household, they would request that the family bring two freshly laid eggs to the sick person's bedside. The lead healer, usually the elder Heepah, would then sit beside the patient and begin the ritualistic chanting and gestures. Meanwhile, Schem would conduct an interview with the family to gather more information about the illness and its symptoms.

Schem took out some herbs she had brought with her and crushed them with mortar and pestle and asked for hot water. She let the herbs soak and then turned to the sick. Heepah had continued humming her chants, eyes closed and both hands on her knees and facing down. She was in a trance, and it would appear, unaware or uninterested in anything else. As Schem approached and put both her hands above the patient, Heepah's humming turned to a chant, and in perfect synchroneity, Schem joined. Schem would spend about five minutes with both hands over the abdomen, holding her hands steady as the chants continued.

By that time, the family and members of the rancheria had gathered around the simple home and patiently waited as the medicine women performed their work. Inside the house, Schem reached for one of the eggs. The use for the second egg is unclear, but it is thought that if one of the eggs was not right, for some unknown reason, the second would be used. The chant never stops and she begins to rub the egg on the

patient's forehead and eventually through every inch of the body. Schem never touched the body, only the egg.

The patient usually remains still during the process. If they're experiencing extreme pain, Schem prepares a special herbal mixture and has them drink it before proceeding with the egg passing ritual. Once the healer finishes passing the egg, they reach for a cup, break the egg, and promptly hand it to Heepah. At this point, the chanting abruptly stops. Heepah then examines the egg, which serves as a vessel for the spirit to manifest and reveal the underlying cause of the patient's sickness, including whether it's the result of a spell or curse.

In some cases, Heepah saw no bewitching. She then would grease her hands with lard and salt before rubbing the patient's belly, starting with her thumbs right under the ribcage. She would work her way around the belly, where her thumbs start from the belly button out and cover the area of the abdomen. Some patients would find this movement painful and would show discomfort. *"Kawik ma'a achik, ipa' ma'a kasa'a,"* said Heepah, indicating that it will be better tomorrow.

Heepah then grasped the patient's waist, just above the hipbones, and began a gentle, downward rub-down motion, tracing the edge of the bones with her palms and fingers all the way to the pelvis. She repeats this soothing motion several times. Next, the healer would instruct the patient to lie on their stomach, and continue the rub-down, targeting specific pressure points on the back and muscles. The patient is given the concoction Schem had prepared earlier to drink and the healing exercise would end.

If Heepah read a spell in the egg, the chanting procedure would continue for hours with the intent to return the bewitching back to the source. This is the way of the spirit. Schem lit dried salvia and spread the smoke over the patient. And again, the end of the healing exercise was marked by the patient drinking the tea. Schem ordered the cracked egg to remain near the patient for a week.

Heepah and Schem

The journey to Heepah and Schem's rancheria was not a long one, but it was filled with excitement and anticipation. Paddy had always admired the healers, who were once respected by the Yuma people. Paddy had witnessed their amazing abilities to cure diseases, soothe pains, and reveal mysteries. He had also learned much from them about the spirit world, the natural forces, and the ancient lore of the ancestors.

Pelon had never met the healers before, but he was eager to do so. Paddy had shared stories about them during their ride, and he was curious about their knowledge and skills. He hoped they could teach him something new, or at least confirm some of his own intuitions and insights. He also wanted to show them his respect and gratitude, for they had helped many people over the years.

Paddy rode horseback, and Pelon followed on one of the mules. The mules were packed with bags of grain; Pelon guessed they were maize, wheat and chickpeas. As they approached the rancheria, they saw smoke rising from a fire and saw where the path, which veered off from the main wagon trail, led toward their place. They followed the path. The pair also heard the clucking of chickens and the barking of dogs. They slowed down their horses and looked around. A small cluster of houses made of reeds and mud, surrounded by a fence of branches and acacia thorns were about. They saw a few people walking in from the fields and could also see planted corn around the rancheria. Other folk were sitting under the shade of mesquite trees and smoking tobacco. They saw children running and playing, laughing and shouting.

They spotted Heepah and Schem's house, which was slightly larger and at the center of the others. It had fabric for windows and doors. Meat was hanging from the porch to dry, and maize kernels spread on mats to roast. They saw a large grinding stone and a pot of boiling water. Schem kneeled on the ground, milling maize on the rock with a cylindrical grinding tool. She was a middle-aged woman, with long black hair and brown skin. Schem wore a dress of cotton cloth and colorful necklaces of shells and beads. Her face tattoos showed lines that went across her cheeks and three lines that went from her bottom lip down to her throat. She looked up and saw the visitors. Schem smiled and waved at them. She put down her grinding rock and stood up. Schem walked toward them, wiping her hands on her apron.

Heepah was sitting outside their house, on a low stool. She was an old woman who's skin showed ware and wrinkles. Both Heepah and Schem used black sediment as treatment for their hair, which always looked black. Heepah wore a shawl of wool and a cotton apron. She had a cane by her side and a pipe in her mouth. She looked calm and serene, as if she knew everything that was happening around her. Heepah didn't open her eyes when she heard the visitors. She smiled and nodded at them. She took out her pipe and put it on the stool. Heepah then stood up, leaning on her cane. She walked toward them, slowly but steadily. You could make out her face tattoos among her wrinkled face, similar to those of Schem's. She had dashed lines that ran down her cheekbones, and they are hard to follow within her wrinkles.

The visitors dismounted and tied the horses to a post. Paddy greeted Schem with a hug and a kiss. They greeted each other and exchanged pleasantries-all in the Yuma dialect. He asked about her health and her work. He complimented her on her home and her chickens. Paddy thanked her for her hospitality and her kindness.

Paddy greeted Heepah with reverence. He bowed his head and touched her hands. She drew Paddy toward her and hugged the man.

As Paddy hugged Heepah, she whispered in his ear, "I'm glad you came, my child. You brought something special for me."

Paddy responded in Yuma tongue, "I brought you some gifts, but what special gift are you referring to?"

Heepah said, "With you is a young man and the coyote spirit greets me before him. This young man will bring balance to the desert and protection to many."

Paddy looked at Pelon, who stood behind him. He wondered what Heepah meant by her words. He felt a surge of curiosity and admiration for the old healer. He said, "You have a gift of vision, Heepah. You can see things that others can't. Please tell me more."

Heepah smiled. "Come sit down, Paddy. I will tell you everything you want to know. But first, let us eat and drink. We have a long night ahead of us."

Heepah and Schem welcomed them with warmth and generosity. They invited them to sit in the shade and share a meal. They told them to make themselves comfortable and feel at home. The healers were happy and honored to have them as their guests.

Paddy and Pelon unloaded the mules and gifted the grain to Schem. They did the same with the two milking goats, to which Schem was more than happy with the gift. That evening they ate lamb, corn cakes and succotash.

As the men prepared for camp, Paddy asked Pelon if he was going to be good staying with the healers. He would be gone for six months but will be back afterwards and take him on a hunt. Pelon felt he would be fine with the women, and he wanted to earn more time with Paddy. He smiled and agreed.

Black Sediment

Early the next morning, Schem and Pelon journeyed to a small lake branching off from the Colorado River. Their path took them along game trails, passing through small valleys and crossing dry creeks nestled among the undulating hills. By the time they reached the lake, the hills had turned a striking red hue. The water lay still, and the lake appeared shallow. A frozen haze brought by dawn still lingered. It was early spring, 1858, and the lake teemed with various birds, including shorebirds, ducks, and egrets. Pelon regretted not having his sling to bring back some plump ducks. Though Schem had brought a basket, its purpose remained unclear to Pelon.

Schem asked Pelon to go in the water and find black sediment. Pelon now understood they were looking for the sediment that is used to treat traditional braids. He remembered wearing it before his hair was cut and going out to the river with his family to retrieve it. But he was young; it was just a game for him back then, and he didn't remember exactly how to find it. Pelon hesitated, as he touched the water with his foot. He quickly jumped back. The water was cold as ice! It felt like a thousand needles piercing his skin. He jerked back and looked at Schem, who laughed at his reaction. Pelon joined her in laughter. "It's really cold!" he said, his laughter turning into a nervous one.

"Do you want to go in?" she asked.

"Not really!" returned Pelon.

Schem spoke to him in a gentle but firm voice. "It is normal to listen to your body. Your body says 'no, don't go in there, it's too cold for you.' It is your body telling you to be afraid of the pain. Be afraid, be afraid, your body doesn't think-you think, but it tells you, be afraid! This will happen many times in your life and the greatest tool a warrior can have is the ability to determine what you can and can't do and what you should really fear; which fear to face and when to walk away. You have to understand that becoming strong is not just about toughening up your body, it's about taming your body with mind and spirit."

"You should have a conversation with your spirit and let it guide you. When you learn to control your breath and calm your heart, you're not just preparing for cold water, you're learning to quiet the storm inside. You will let your mind take over. Only when you stop paying all mind to your body, you will be able to listen. It is meditation but with a purpose. You'll discover that your body is deceiving you this time — that you are capable of entering the water. And the pain that brings the cold is nothing.

"By focusing your mind and gradually walking into the water, you're testing your willpower, discipline, and faith. You're proving to yourself that you can overcome any obstacle, regardless of its discomfort. When you finally immerse yourself in the ice-cold water, you'll feel the intense cold against your skin. At the same time, you'll be washing away your fears, doubts, and limitations.

"Now, go in and find the black sediment and bring it to me."

Pelon listened intently and found his mind fully engaged and relaxed at the same time. Schem's words and her delivery had a hypnotic effect on him. He found it easy to separate his physical being from a higher self. "I have been in cold water before," he thought. As Pelon was deep in thought, he looked up in the sky and time stood still; he could see a coyote joining them from afar and somehow urging him on, "...I see you, great coyote."

Pelon felt her words also inspire him, as if they were awakening something deep within. He realized that he was not really afraid of the water, that he was brave. He decided to challenge himself, to prove to himself that he could do it.

He slowly made his way to the water. As he stepped in, he easily ignored the cold that bit his flesh. It was just above his knees in depth. He then knelt and dug into the mud, looking for the black sediment that Schem wanted. His body was mostly submerged, only his face was dry. Pelon felt the water burn his skin, but he continued paying no mind. He fought back shivers with deep breaths. He dug around him and lifted the soil out of the water. Not dark enough. He kept moving around and within fifteen minutes, he found the right color, consistency and smell. This sediment felt like boiled bone broth when it gets cold, not exactly like lard, yet not exactly solid. Pelon brought it to her. She nodded and smiled, and he went back for more. He repeated this until he filled the basket with the dark soil.

"Master your mind, body, and spirit. You're becoming a warrior, a seeker of truth, and a force of nature," Schem said.

Pelon felt the cold water invigorate him, washing away his doubts and fears. He smiled and asked, "Can you do my hair too?"

She laughed with him and agreed, and they headed back to the rancheria.

Back at the rancheria, Paddy cinched his saddle and prepared his mules for departure, and Heepah accompanied him. "Pelon will be staying here to help you out."

"I know," she replied. She didn't show her eyes, but Paddy sensed they would be filled with sadness, resolve and alas understanding. He enveloped her in a warm embrace; arms to shoulders and foreheads touching, she whispered, "May the road rise up to meet you, dear one." As they parted, he pressed six glinting silver coins into her palm.

Heepah's demeaner faltered as soon as the coins touched her skin. She gently pushed his hand away. "No, Paddy, I have no need for these. They bring only darkness and desire. I've seen it consume men's souls, turning them against each other like ravenous beasts. It starts with a single coin, a small invitation, and soon the hunger devours them whole." Her voice dropped to a whisper. "Don't let it into your heart, Paddy. It will take everything in its path. You must carry this burden, not me. And in your future, and your future's future will carry the burden of saving men's souls from the grasp of this metal."

Paddy's eyes locked onto her face, and he felt the weight of her words settle upon him like a mantle. She felt his stare and gave him a loving smile. With a nod, he accepted the coins, tucking them into his saddlebag as a reminder of Heepah's wisdom and the perils that lay ahead.

Sneaking Up

Paddy was excited with anticipation, as he approached the familiar landscape of Yuma. The setting sun cast a golden hue over the rugged terrain. Six months have passed since he had last seen Pelon and the others, and he couldn't wait to share the adventures that awaited them.

As Paddy rode into the rancheria, he saw Pelon standing tall and proud. No longer a child, Pelon had grown considerably, now towering over Paddy with a newfound strength and confidence. The boy he had left behind had transformed into a young man, ready to face the challenges of the world.

"Paddy!" Pelon shouted, his voice deeper and more resonant than before. He ran to embrace his old friend, the camaraderie between them unbroken by time.

"Pelon, you've grown so much! You were just a little lad last, I seen ya'!" Paddy said, marveling at the changes in the young man. "I've returned as promised. Are you ready?"

Pelon's eyes sparkled with excitement. "Always ready, Paddy."

Paddy then greeted Schem with a hearty handshake and after a reverence, enveloped Heepah in a warm embrace. The joy of reunion was evident in their eyes. As Pelon led Paddy's horse to the water and feeding trough, he couldn't help but notice the chestnut mare that followed. His heart skipped a beat — Ruby! With a broad grin, he quickly unloaded the grain bags and stowed them in the grain shed, before tenderly removing Ruby's saddle and bridle.

Pelon felt around Ruby's head and under her jaw, looking for any injury or abnormality. He had learned to do this examination while working at the livery. With a gentle touch, he opened Ruby's mouth, and a warm breath wafted out. He slipped his fingers inside, feeling the smooth enamel of her teeth. The incisors, those front teeth that told so much about a horse's age, were still relatively straight, with only a hint of wear. He realized that she was a young adult, likely between 4-10 years old.

As he explored further, he noticed the canines, those distinctive teeth on either side of the incisors, were still small and neatly aligned. The molars, too, showed minimal wear, their surfaces still bearing the slight ridges of youth. This horse had barely begun to scratch the surface of adulthood.

He ran his fingers over the teeth again, feeling for any signs of uneven wear or misalignment. But all seemed well in this young mouth — the teeth were clean, the gums healthy, and the overall structure sound. He closed the horse's mouth, patting its neck in approval.

"Well, Ruby," he whispered, "you're growing up strong and healthy. Keep those teeth clean, and you'll be smiling bright for years to come." The horse nickered softly, as if it understood, and he couldn't help but smile at its vibrant spirit. Pelon continued to pass the palms of his hands through the entirety of the horse. Feeling for any injury and keeping an eye on Ruby's reactions. She will tell him if there's any pain. When he got to the tail, he grabbed it and gave it a slight tug toward him. Her balance was good and she feels no pain. The last check was over each leg and down to the hoof, where he took an opportunity to clean the inside. Pelon continued pampering Ruby as the adults caught up in conversation.

The following months unfolded like a vivid tapestry of adventure under the crisp autumn skies. Paddy and Pelon delved into the heart of the wilderness, their spirits soaring with each new discovery. They treaded ancient game trails, hunting deer and sheep, their skills sharpened with every hunt. Paddy imparted the delicate art of tracking to Pelon, teaching him to read the subtle signs left by animals and the silent patience of a true hunter.

This hunt was not Pelon's first. He had joined many parties with his people. But his duty was of an apprentice, staying far from the older hunters.

Pelon crouched behind a boulder in the Chocolate Mountains of southern California. The sun rose over the desert landscape, casting a warm glow across the rugged terrain. He had been scouting these mountains for weeks, searching for the elusive bighorn sheep.

Pelon's gaze swept across the rocky outcroppings and scrubby desert vegetation. He knew the ram's habits, its favorite grazing spots and watering holes. He had spent countless hours studying the terrain, learning the subtle signs of the ram's presence.

Paddy waited downhill of the action. Pelon had followed the ram's trail and spotted fresh scat. As he waited, Pelon's senses came alive. He felt the gentle breeze rustling his hair, the warmth of the sun on his skin, and the silence of the desert broken only by the occasional bird call. He was one with the landscape, attuned to the subtle vibrations of the wild.

Suddenly, he spotted a ghostly figure — a large ram, its coat a mesmerizing blend of brown and white, blending seamlessly into the surrounding landscape. Pelon's heart quickened as he observed the ram's behavior. It was grazing, its ears perked up, alert to any sign of danger.

Without making a sound, Pelon began to stalk the ram, using the natural terrain to conceal himself. Pelon thought of Paddy's words, "If you can sneak up on a ram, you can sneak up on any man." He moved slowly, deliberately, his eyes fixed on the ram's position. The wind was in his favor, carrying the scent of creosote and mesquite away from the ram's sensitive nose.

As Pelon closed in, he noticed the ram's body language — its ears twitching, its eyes scanning the horizon. He froze, holding his breath, as the ram's gaze swept over him. For what felt like an eternity, the two locked eyes, the only sound the gentle rustling of the desert breeze.

The ram, seemingly satisfied that the coast was clear, returned to its grazing. Pelon let out a silent sigh of relief, his muscles relaxing as he continued to observe the ram.

He waited for what felt like hours, the sun beating down on his back, until the ram began to move toward a nearby cluster of rocks. Pelon knew this was his chance. He slowly rose from his crouched position, his bow and arrow at the ready.

With a steady hand, Pelon drew the string back, his arrow fixed on the ram's vitals. He took a deep breath, focusing on the shot. The arrow flew straight and true, striking the ram with a soft thud.

The ram crumpled to the ground, tried to get up, aware of its pending demise. Pelon approached the ram, his heart swelling with respect and gratitude. He had outsmarted the ghostly ram, and in doing so, had earned a deep appreciation for the majestic creature. "Thank you, brother ram, for providing with your meat. Have a good journey." He covered the ram's eyes and slit its throat. He measured the ram using the width of his hands and said, "Twelve hands, not bad for a city boy." He had been called that in the past, clearly meant to demean.

Pelon whistled a "coast is clear" at Paddy. Paddy whistled back to indicate "acknowledged." As he field-dressed the ram, Pelon couldn't help but feel a sense of awe for the Chocolate Mountains' rugged beauty and the elusive bighorn sheep that called it home. This was a great feat, he had single-handedly put down a big ram. He knew this hunt would stay with him forever, a testament to the thrill of the chase and the majesty of the wild.

By the time Paddy climbed to Pelon, the internals had been separated. It was still hot out, so he decided to quarter the animal with the skin on and help keep the meat from spoiling. He then salted the exposed flesh before placing in bags. With two of the ram's quarters packed onto his back, Pelon began the arduous journey down the mountain, the desert sun beating down on him. Paddy carried the other two. He knew he'd return to these mountains, drawn by the allure of the ram and the thrill of the hunt. They reached Ruby and Paddy's colt and rode the rest of the way home.

That night, they reached the rancheria. Schem made a salty brine and dipped two quarters after skinning them. As those two quarters soaked, Pelon skinned the other two and filleted the meat. Schem then thoroughly salted the fillets. As she worked on the meat, she talked to the ram. "You were a big boy. Look at your beautiful muscles. We are so glad you found food and lived a happy life..." Schem set a pot with water to boil. She threw in a handful of spices including black pepper, laurel leaves, and garlic. As the water reached the boiling point, she ground two different types of chiles, a bit of cumin seed, and oregano.

As Schem continued to prepare dinner, she had a method of blending the ground spices in the pot. She reached for a simple piece of cotton cloth and created a spice bag. Schem cut a square piece of cloth, about twice the size of her palm, and placed the ground spices — chiles, cumin and oregano — in the center. Then, she gathered the edges of the cloth and tied them together with a piece of twine made from the same cotton cloth, forming a small pouch.

With the spice bag secure, Schem added it to the pot, where it simmered alongside the other ingredients, infusing the dish with a warm, inviting aroma. As the flavors melded together, Pelon could see the spice bag gently swaying in the liquid, releasing its treasures. "It smells so good!" he thought.

When it was time to serve, she simply spooned out the spice bag and discarded the spent spices, leaving behind a deliciously seasoned meal without any fuss. The cotton cloth had done its job perfectly, containing the spices and making clean-up a breeze. Pelon smiled, knowing he'd learned this simple yet effective technique.

While the stew soon was at a low boil. Schem brought out a coveted bottle filled with wine vinegar. It was not very common around these parts, and she used three tablespoons for the pot of meat. It cooked for another hour, and then they feasted.

There Once Were Giants

Pelon's belly was full, and he was happy. No longer did he feel that he was an impetuous boy. He didn't feel at the back of the hunting party anymore. Pelon could now enjoy the quiet and ponder wisdom instilled by his mentors. After dinner, Paddy and Pelon camped near the river, and as they enjoyed a fire, they were able to see the reflection of a pair of eyes looking back at them from deep in the trees. They both turned to look at the eyes, then looked back at each other. The eyes were about eight feet from the ground. Pelon said, "That is brother racoon. A man's eye doesn't reflect light, and it's too tall."

Paddy nodded his head. He took a pause, which he does this before sharing wisdom. As the campfire crackled, Paddy recounted an old tale. Pelon listened intently, the flickering flames casting shadows on his face.

"Pelon, your people come from a stock of very large men, very strong, yet very gentle men. It was the year 1540, and Coronado was the Governor of Nueva Galicia. Nueva Galicia are the western states that later became part of Mexico, including Aguascalientes, Guanajuato, Colima, Jalisco, Nayarit and Zacatecas. Francisco Vazquez de Coronado was the governor of that territory, and he was a man driven by the promise of untold riches of the legendary Seven Cities of Cibola.

Paddy paused, his eyes reflecting the firelight. "Coronado set out from Compostella, in the current state of Nayarit, and ventured into the harsh lands of Sonora. They called it Senora back then. His journey took him through places the likes of Valle de los Corazones and San Miguel de Culiacan. But the land was unforgiving, and they found little food.

"Now, here's where the tale takes a turn." Paddy's voice grew more animated. "Captain Rodrigo Maldonado and a small group broke away from the main party, following a nameless westward river to the seacoast, where a ship awaited them with provisions. I believe this river was the Gila. There, they encountered peoples unlike any they'd seen before. The river people they encountered were giants. The tallest of his men only reached their chest. Two hundred years ago, this land was filled with giants."

Pelon leaned in closer, captivated by the story. "What happened to the giants?"

"News of this finding made it straight to the Viceroy of New Spain, Don Antonio de Mendoza y Pacheco. The explorers had a process to handle these findings, for they had encountered giants in the past. They had done away with them in the Caribbean, South America, and other places. I believe they employ the remaining arm of the templar knights. These were warriors from 500 years past. Their only job today being to hunt down and exterminate giants of the Americas."

"The Viceroy then wrote a letter back to the Old World. It read something like this:

"Most Honorable Lord, The 4th Earl of Caithness, George Sinclair V

"In the year of our Savior Jesus Christ 1540, Francisco Vazquez de Coronado, Governor of Nueva Galicia, led an expedition in search of the Seven Cities of Cibola as so fixed and arranged by my own person. Given that they did find the countries in which he searched for but did not find the riches. And after this has been made they came to understand the direction and localities in which they had traveled and the borders of the vast country they had at hand.

"So it was sought to make of the Seven Cities of Cibola known, then this land known as Senora traversed by Governor Vazques de Coronado. His journey began in Compostella, some 110 leagues from Mexico. The Governor gone into this land by the way of Valle de los Corazones, some 120 leagues form San Miguel de Culiacan and when travelling into this providence found great scarcity of victuals. North of the baren countries of Senora and following an unnamed westward river to the seacoast, Captain Rodrigo Maldonado and a small force had separated from the main party and faced ungodly creatures, the likes of which previous encounters have been recorded in Curazao and the Patagonias.

"As it has been God's providence to defeat and annihilate these creatures in battle and that has been described by Bernardo Claraval's Liber Ad Milites Templi de Laude Novae

Militiae to be held true today. My Lordship, it is for this reason emissaries on my behalf have sought you and brought you this letter, for there is no other order or guild that is so ordained by God that may rid these countries of such evil. It has been great feats of bravery where in my lifetime the Holy Warriors delivered a swift and absolute end to the giants of Curazao and to the eclipsing monsters of Patagonia, it is now the time to ensure safe pilgrimage through the land of the Yuma giants.

"*My Lordship, it is well known that the Knights of Christ neither rage, want or desire glory but seek to strike down evil, charge into battle aiming to elevate your soul and to have a good death. In so, pacify this land of evil once and for all.*

"*Signed, Don Antonio de Mendoza y Pacheco Viceroy of New Spain*"

Paddy's performance was remarkably realistic. He even altered his accent, now sounding like a Spaniard. As Paddy concluded his narrative, a hush seemed to descend on the night, the gravity of the story enveloping them. Pelon chose to reflect on what he comprehended and remain vigilant for nuances the next time Paddy recounts this tale. Closing his eyes, Pelon dreamt of the Yuma giants.

The next day, Pelon looked at Paddy with renewed respect, understanding that the lessons he learned from his mentor were steeped in the wisdom of ages past. The bond between them deepened, their shared stories and adventures forging a connection that would guide them through many more journeys to come. Each day was a lesson, each night a story shared under the glittering canopy of stars, their bond deepening with the promise of more adventures to come.

Paddy shared his knowledge of geology, teaching Pelon how to identify various rocks and minerals. They explored potential mine claims, their eyes ever watchful for veins of precious metal hidden within the earth. Paddy's experience and Pelon's youthful curiosity made them an unstoppable team, each discovery fueling their desire for more.

Pelon learned to handle Paddy's Colt six-shooter. He practiced drawing it every day, and Paddy allowed him to fire three shots daily. Pelon would set up tin cans on large rocks, draw his gun, cock the hammer, and aim. He practiced this sequence twenty times before firing a shot. Paddy would discuss with Pelon the importance of deciding to shoot someone before drawing his weapon. "If you haven't made the decision to shoot a man, keep your gun in its holster, lad." As they sat by the campfire at night under the twinkling stars, they spoke of their dreams, aspirations, and the future that awaited them. Pelon asked if he could join Paddy on one of his prospecting adventures, to which Paddy agreed.

Winter approached, and Paddy knew it was time to return to Tucson. "Pelon, I must go back to Tucson," he said one crisp morning as they packed up their campsite. "But you will stay here with Heepah and Schem. There is still much for you to learn from them."

Pelon nodded, appreciating Paddy's advice. "I will remain here. But will you return?"

"And we will enjoy ourselves more," Paddy assured, gripping Pelon's shoulder. "This isn't the end, just a break. Stay strong, my lad. And take good care of Ruby!"

"I won't eat her," Pelon replied, and they both laughed.

After a final embrace, Paddy rode away, leaving Pelon in the care of Heepah and Schem. The young man watched until Paddy was just a dot on the horizon, feeling a new sense of purpose. He knew that the knowledge and skills he acquired would equip him for the trials ahead, and he eagerly anticipated the day when he and Paddy would set off on their grand adventures again.

Becoming an Observer

This winter has been extraordinarily cold and wet. Two storms have produced powerful surges of water around the rancheria, the second one had a wash branch out unexpectedly and took half of the homestead. After that second storm, it was necessary to move Heepah and Schem west, toward the rocky foothills and away from the river. There was an old circular hut, and Pelon made it habitable again in a short time. The camp was now at a higher elevation, with a better view of the valley but further from the water. He also made new stalls for the milk goats, and the chickens stayed inside with Heepah and Schem for now.

The first few nights Pelon had a difficult time sleeping. He kept dreaming that he was chasing a rabbit out in the desert, but despite his effort, it always got away. And that would wake Pelon up in the middle of the night with his heart feeling like it wants to jump out of his body.

Pelon finally told Grandma Heepah about his trouble sleeping and about the dream. She asked about his stomach, how it has been lately, and he told her his stomach felt fine. She then said, "Tonight, you stop running and become the hunter." These words resonated in Pelon's head all day long. He decided to give it a try.

That night, Pelon built a larger fire, and sat before it to clear his mind before sleeping. The thoughts remained in his head for a while. Thoughts of Ruby, if she was feeling comfortable in her new home, about Heepah and Schem and how they will endure this cold and would he go ride with Paddy in a few weeks. He was shaking his rattle, which he had taken from a large snake last summer. She had fourteen rings on her. Pelon sang the hymns of the ancestors and shook the rattle with a rhythm. His skin was getting hot from the fire, but as Pelon continued the chant, his mind drifted from that place and for a moment, he could see himself sitting by the fire and performing the chant. Pelon was outside of his body.

Last spring, Pelon went to his first Karuk (which has also been spelled *Kerook*) at the request of Grandma Heepah. That

experience helped him with many things, but it also taught him about moments when he leaves his body. Upon arrival at this Karuk, Pelon greeted the elders and one asked, "Eh-Pelo, why are you here?"

Without much thought, he answered, "I'm here for the Karuk."

The elder repeated, "Eh-Pelo, why are you here?"

This time, Pelon was deeply contemplative. Why am I here? None of the answers seemed adequate. Why attend the Karuk? Why be in the river? Why exist in this life? His only response was, "I don't know." The elder then opened his right hand, raised his palm and made a welcoming gesture. That week changed Pelon.

Pelon is now more comfortable being an observer. His ancestors were better at it, and he now believes this is something that needs to be taught to the young ones. Pelon can see the desert moon casting its silvery glow upon the arid landscape, and he was curious to look around. Within seconds, he was away from the foothills and back in the desert. As Pelon prowled through the sandy dunes, his paws barely made a sound on the rocky terrain. Pelon realizes he has paws... he was connected with the coyote spirit. His nose twitched with every sniff, drinking in the scent of creosote and mesquite. Pelon reveled in the freedom of the open range, his heart racing with excitement.

Pelon calmed his heart and became the hunter, just as Heepah had recommended. He then spotted a plump rabbit nibbling on a cactus flower, and his ears perked up. He crouched low, tail twitching, as he observed his prey. This time, he looked around and located her hole. The rabbit, oblivious to the danger lurking mere yards away, continued to graze. Pelon salivated at the thought of the hunt.

With lightning-fast reflexes, he sprang into action, dashing toward the rabbit with a burst of speed. The chase was on! His paws pounded the earth as he gained ground. The rabbit darted toward its burrow, but Pelon anticipated its move, positioning himself between the hole and his quarry.

Undeterred, the rabbit made a break for the open desert. Pelon gave chase. As he closed in, the rabbit's instincts kicked into high gear. She suddenly froze, her paws locked in place, as she assessed the danger mere inches from her quivering whiskers. In that split second, she plotted her escape.

With a burst of adrenaline, she shifted her weight onto her powerful hind legs, preparing to unleash her evasive maneuver. Her front legs remained still, serving as a pivot point as she rotated her body around them.

In a flash, she swiveled her hips, generating torque and propelling herself in a sharp, new direction. The ground beneath her feet blurred, as she pushed off with her hind legs, exploding into a sprint. Her agility and flexibility allowed her to make a tight, smooth turn, dodging my outstretched jaws by mere inches. As she gained speed, her paws pounded the earth in a blur, her little heart racing with fear and determination.

The chase was far from over, but the rabbit's lightning-fast reflexes and cunning had given her a slim lead. She darted and weaved, using every trick in the book to shake her pursuer. Pelon took his chance and anticipated her next move. She jumped right into his mouth, Pelon's jaws snapping shut and securing the catch. He had caught his prize!

As Pelon stood victorious, the desert landscape unfolded before him like a canvas of endless possibility. He felt the rush of the hunt, the thrill of the catch, and the satisfaction of a meal well-earned. The moon above seemed to smile upon his triumph, casting a silver glow over the desert's vast expanse.

In that moment, Pelon was one with the land, a true coyote, ruler of the arid realm. His howl echoed through the night, a triumphant cry that sent shivers down the spines of all who heard it. He was the desert's apex predator, and this was his domain.

The Great Flood of 1862

The next day, Pelon felt well rested and full of vigor. He saddled Ruby and said his goodbyes to Heepah and Schem. Pelon had to start his travel toward Tucson to *rendezvous* with Paddy. They'll be spending most of next year working on mine projects and Pelon will provide as much help as Paddy needs.

The winter storms had just ravaged Colorado City, bringing with it torrential rains that caused the Colorado River to overflow its banks. The resulting floodwaters swept through the town, destroying homes and businesses, leaving chaos in their wake.

At the local livery, owner Paco was beside himself — five of his prized horses had broken free during the tempest and were now lost in the desert. The usually tranquil desert landscape was transformed into a treacherous expanse of mud, water and debris.

Paco gathered his most trusted hands, cowboys Alex and Ryan, and asked Pelon to join him. Paco has been a good friend, and Pelon was happy to help. Together, they set out to find the missing horses, braving the unforgiving terrain and residual floodwaters.

Paco and Ryan rode west past the limits of Arizona City and down the mesa into the old Colorado City. This area was still flooded. Ruins of some homesteads remained, while others were completely washed away. Paco and Ryan were determined to find their way through the thicket of mesquite trees. They would follow the mesquite forest, as it turned south toward Sumner's Camp, looking for tracks and asking people. It took them most of the day to reach Sumner's Camp. The town was deserted, and they found no trace of Paco's horses. From Sumner's Camp, they headed east and up the sandy mesa. Most of the folk from down in the valley had made camp there and again, no sign of the horses.

Alex and Pelon moved south following the general direction of the storm. As they entered the sandy desert, the fierce wind and frigid rain struck their faces. It was a challenging task since all the trails had been washed away, leaving no clear indication of where the horses had gone. Leading the way, Pelon asked Ruby, "where would you go if you were scared?" while continuing to scan the terrain for any signs of the horses. Alex kept close behind, his eyes scanning the horizon.

Unable to locate any trails, Pelon paused and looked around. All they could see was desert bush. The cold air numbed Pelon's nose, as he took a deep breath. The sky was overcast, but there was a gap through which sun rays pierced the misty horizon and reached the ground. Pelon figured that would be a good direction to follow.

Halfway toward the light clearing, Pelon suddenly stopped and focused on the ground. "Here," he whispered, pointing to a faint hoof print in the muddy soil. "They passed through here, heading south." The tracks indeed led toward the sunlight.

They followed the tracks slowly and deliberately. Despite the storm having erased much of the trail, he knew to stay on course, guided by ancestral wisdom from the sky. Navigating through the flood-damaged landscape, they encountered uprooted mesquite trees, washed-out arroyos, and other wood debris. After hours of searching, they finally saw something in the distance — a group of horses huddled together for warmth in a patch of sunlight.

With excitement, Alex spurred his horse forward, but Pelon cautioned him to approach slowly. As we got closer, we confirmed these were the livery horses, shivering and frightened but alive.

Pelon released Ruby's reins and let her take over. She approached the other horses with familiarity, calming them and allowing us to get near. With gentle words and soothing gestures, we calmed the horses and checked each one for injuries. Once assured they were ready to travel, Pelon asked Alex to start the journey back to Arizona City, promising to catch up soon with Ruby.

Pelon stopped at some downed trees and started snapping branches. Everything was wet, but he listened for the dry snap of the dry inner wood. Knowing they need to head back before nightfall, Pelon gathered twigs and resinous bark, made bundles tied with ripped strips from his shirt dipped in silty mud. These bundles were tied together and in his saddle bags.

Ruby and Pelon quickly caught up to Alex and the horses. They had been riding for less than an hour when the sun set, leaving them in darkness and without any moonlight. Pelon dismounted Ruby and walked until he couldn't retrace their steps anymore. It was time to use one of the torches. After lighting it, they got back on track. The fog descended along with the night, reducing their visibility to just a few feet ahead. The first torch burned out quickly, lasting perhaps half an hour. They lit the second torch and continued their journey. They covered around two miles before the second torch died, which put them in a difficult situation.

Camping was not an option due to the cold and the challenge of finding dry wood. Pelon decided to let Ruby lead the way since the livery was her home from birth, and she knew it well. He released her reins, allowing Ruby to move from a walk to a light trot. It was a cautious trot, keeping her hooves close to the ground but gaining speed. Pelon could see nothing, so he clung tightly to his saddle. Alex and the other horses followed closely. Within minutes, Pelon detected the faint smell of smoke — they were getting close! Despite their fear of riding without seeing where they were going, Pelon felt confident that they were on the right path. Ruby trotted another two miles in a span of about ten minutes, and soon Pelon saw faint signs of fires ahead. Pelon patted Ruby, gradually took the reins, and slowed her down. They made it!

As they rode into town, Paco had returned from Sumner Camp earlier and greeted them with relief. "Thank you, boys, I owe you one," he said, patting the horses' necks. "Paco, today we had help from our ancestors, who guided Ruby."

Covert Copper

Charles Poston, a staunch Union supporter, sat in the dimly lit back room of his adobe home, his eyes scanning the horizon for any signs of movement. His friend, William H. Burke, slipped in quietly, carrying a large, rolled piece of hide, and casting furtive glances behind him, making sure he wasn't followed.

"Charles, I've got a plan that could change everything for the Union," Paddy whispered, unrolling the deerskin on the table with a sense of urgency.

Poston's eyes narrowed as he scrutinized the detailed survey of the eastern mountains. "What is this, Paddy? Another mining scheme?"

Burke leaned closer, his voice barely audible. "Precisely. We can extract gold, lead and copper from these hills near the Salty River. The Union's desperate for this metal, and we stand ready to supply them covertly. The profits will not only bolster our cause but also discreetly support our own needs."

Poston's face lit with a mixture of excitement and caution. "By the desert stars, Paddy, this could be monumental. But we must proceed with the utmost secrecy. There's more to it than mining the metals. Pertaining to the copper, we have to crush, separate, roast and smelt into ingots prior to transport. Then we must move it back through California, since heading east is not an option. No, I'm not saying it's impossible, but it will likely be expensive!"

"You might as well call it impossible, Charles, ain't no side of this plan that looks pretty. But I can't fight this war with me body anymore, and by St. Christopher, I will use me wits and wealth in its place! I share this claim with Peralta near the four peaks, and he's all lined up. The mining part is me business, ye know I can be trusted to put the right people to work, find me a way to the Glamis station, preferably in small teams. Maybe four or five loaded wagons at a time. Find me a safe way to Glamis and once on the train, the metals will be safe. Let's get to work, quietly and efficiently."

And so, the two friends embarked on their ambitious venture. Paddy, with his expertise in mining, began assessing the location for copper deposits. Poston, with his business acumen, handled logistics and financing. In fact, Poston had ties to President Lincoln himself, and recently had traveled to

Washington, D.C. Together, they assembled a team of skilled miners, many of whom were Union sympathizers, eager to contribute to the war effort.

Pelon had arrived earlier in the month and went ahead of Paddy to the four peaks. His job is to keep an eye on the mine workers and prevent any spies from foiling their plan. For now, Pelon disappeared into the night, a ghostly figure guarding the mine's interests.

Over the ensuing months, the mining venture prospered. Within a four-square-mile area, they operated five distinct mines. Poston and Burke reinvested their profits into the Union cause, and they ensured that the approximately 60 mine workers were well-equipped and provisioned. The copper production was substantial, with over ten tons of ingots ready for shipment. Similarly, five tons of lead were queued for dispatch. Gold was also refined in the shared smelter, with an undisclosed quantity swiftly transported back to Tucson on a pony team as soon as it was poured. Although Paddy and Poston kept this information confidential, within a few months, the gold revenue was fully sustaining the operation.

The mining camp was accessible via a single wagon trail. Supplies were delivered bi-weekly and dropped off at the entrance loading dock. At the camp's entrance stood a guard shack, manned continuously by one of Chato's men. Right past the guard shack, the path divides: The left fork leads to the mines and toward the river, while the right fork directs to the charcoal production area.

From the outset, Pelon had been monitoring the operations discretely. Apart from Paddy and the mine's head of security, Chato, an older but stout man, no one was aware of Pelon's presence. He maintained a distant camp, living off the land by trapping rabbits and fishing in the Salt River.

One evening, Pelon stood atop a rocky outcropping, gazing out over the mining camp. He looked at the sky, and one particular cloud caught his attention. It had the shape of a rabbit. For a moment he was reminded of chasing a rabbit in his dreams. *It's time to hunt,* he thought. His eyes scanned the dusty terrain, searching for any sign of suspicious activity. The setting sun cast long shadows, perfect cover for clandestine meetings. As he surveyed the area, Pelon's attention settled on a lone figure slipping away from the camp. The miner, James, had been acting strangely all day. Pelon's instincts kicked in; he knew he had to follow. Pelon descended from his vantage point, keeping a safe distance from James. He tracked the miner through the scrubby desert vegetation, using the fading light to conceal himself.

James led Pelon to a valley between the rolling hills, in a secluded arroyo, where a figure waited in the shadows. Pelon recognized the spot — an ideal location for a secret meeting. Pelon crept closer, using the dry riverbed's natural camouflage. He didn't wear any shoes or boots; his steps continued with minimal noise. Even the crunch of gravel beneath his feet was tenuous and discreet.

As he approached, Pelon heard hushed voices:

"...We've been storing tons of ingots for weeks now. I heard they'll start moving the metals next week..." James whispered.

The unknown agent's voice was low and gravelly. "What will the escort look like?"

Pelon froze, inches from the meeting spot. He strained to listen, committing every word to memory.

James hesitated before responding, "I don't know about the escort...and it's getting dangerous for me, I need assurance of payment. Give me a drop to help assemble my nerves."

The agent's tone turned menacing.: "You'll get your payment when we get our hands on the metals. You better get yourself on that detail! I'll be back in two days, and you better have something for me!"

Pelon mentally filed away the conversation, noting the agent's Southern drawl. The meeting concluded, and the agent vanished into the darkness. James returned to the camp, unaware of Pelon's surveillance. Pelon retreated, his mind racing with implications. He knew he had stumbled upon something significant. The mining operation's secrecy was compromised; Pelon's work had just begun.

He would report to Chato, advising increased security measures and discreetly investigating James' loyalty. Pelon's expertise in counterintelligence would ensure the mining operation remained secure, protecting its valuable secrets.

Pelon made his way circumventing the mine. There was smoke in all the rolling valleys, a clear indication of the near-

by camp. The mining camp hummed with activity, the workers operated two shifts, and there were always people breaking rock. The recent encounter had confirmed his worst fears: Confederate spies were planning to steal the precious metals. The time for observation was over; now, he had to act.

Returning to his secluded camp, Pelon meticulously mapped out his plan. The key to his strategy lay in Chato, the mine's head of security. Chato was a man of few words, whose loyalty to Paddy was unwavering. Pelon knew that Chato's involvement would be crucial in countering the threat.

As dawn broke, Pelon approached Chato's tent, finding the elderly man already awake, his keen eyes scanning the horizon. Pelon moved his face, signaling him to follow. Chato slapped his holster on and made his way, following Pelon. They darted toward the dark side of the hill, still clinging to the night as the sun began to peek behind it. "Chato, we have a problem," Pelon began, his voice low but urgent. "Confederate spies are planning to steal the metals. We need to take immediate action."

Chato's gaze hardened. "Chinga-o!" He grabbed his big hat, as if it would fly away without his hand. "Can we take 'em on? Tell me more!"

"Don't take your guards for the caravan escort next week. You need to recruit six volunteers from the mine crew today," Pelon continued. "James from Las Cruzes will be eager to participate. He's one of the Confederates."

"Jijo de la chingada! Why don't I just fill this pendejo full of lead?" said Chato, with passion.

"If we kill him now, they'll just seduce another of your workers with the promise of riches. And we'll have to start this business of finding him again. You let him in the escort, treat him no different than the others. And make sure to go over the map with them. The best place to put an ambush for the caravan is right before we leave the mountains. The wagons will be slow like turtles, when they ride the two miles of dry wash and they'll be far enough from camp to make an attack feel safe. And Poston's men will meet the caravan on the main wagon trail, so they won't dare risk attacking the joined forces. Once the caravan has left, you will assemble all of your guards and ride after them. Give them enough time to make it to dry wash before letting yourself known. I will be there before the Confederates and will thin them out for you."

Chato nodded, understanding the gravity of the situation. "Jijo de la chingada! (Chato's hand went up to his hat again) It will be hard to look at that pendejo in the eye and not kill el infeliz, traidor! We put our trust in these people, and you see what happens." Chato took a few seconds to gather his thoughts. "Ok. I'll do it. We have eight men I trust who can follow the wagons."

Chato was not worried a bit about the fight that would ensue. He had been forged in the west at the time it was the wildest. He was angry to find Jame's treachery. It was the worst thing for a man like Chato, to have to kill a man he once considered a friend. He took a big swig of tequila and smoothed out his nerves. He was ready to go.

Operations continued as if normal. Chato went on his business and approached a group of men later that day, where he knew James would be an ear's distance, and asked for volunteers. He offered a full day's pay for every day on the road plus an extra silver piece when they return. Half of the group stood up taking the offer, and James quickly made his way to the front. The six men picked, and they were to report to Chato's tent at the end of their shift. With James in the group, Chato continued to execute his plan without flaws. The trap is ready to be set.

Preparations were in full swing, as Pelon closely observed James, noting every detail of the miner's actions. He understood that the success of his plan depended not only on Chato's men but also on his ability to outsmart the spies. The next night, the agent arrived at the rendezvous point and awaited James. Moving like a shadow, Pelon watched the meeting, as the information was conveyed to the spy as intended.

The weight was balanced among five heavy wagons the day before departure, each pulled by a 12-mule team. Early the next morning, the convoy loaded with copper and lead ingots readied for departure, with Chato assigning tasks to the escort team. The drivers and volunteer guards inspected their weapons, ensuring they were prepared for any potential conflict. By sunrise, the convoy was set to embark.

"Vamonos cabrones!" shouted Chato. And the ride to the Glamis station began.

Leaving the mines was challenging. They first climbed a small hill, then slowly descended to the bottom, where the mules pulled the wagons from the sandy wash. The well-fed mules kept a steady pace. This was repeated for each rolling hill.

Dreaming the Prize

Pelon had reached the foothills. He traveled by night, moving silently. After finding high ground, he waited for two days to observe any activity. It was the best location for an ambush, and the Confederates are sure to select this a valley for their trap. And just as expected they came the night before the caravan was to leave the mine.

From his vantage point, Pelon counted ten men in total. Four were identifiable as Confederate soldiers disguised in regular clothes, while the remaining six appeared to be hired from the local tavern. As the Confederates set up their camp, Pelon returned to his own campsite and took to rest. While heading to the south side of the hill, he nearly stepped on a rattlesnake. As it slithered away, he seized it by its rattler and swiftly snapped it, killing the snake instantly. Lifting the snake, he saw it was about five feet long. *Dinner*, he thought.

The snake was peeled, cooked and eaten quickly. Pelon kept the rattle, skin and the head. He shook the rattle as he prepared white ochre. Once at his camp he comforted Ruby, who had been alone all day. He painted his face, arms, and body. He blew smoke toward his body and asked the spirit for strength and wisdom. He asked his ancestors to be with him on the battlefield. He put out the fire and went to rest.

Pelon settled into his makeshift bed, the cool night air brushing against his face as he pulled his blanket tighter. His body ached from the long day of preparations, and his mind was a whirlwind of strategies and contingencies. But as he closed his eyes, the weight of exhaustion finally took over, and he drifted into a deep sleep.

In the dream, Pelon found himself in a lush, sun-dappled forest. The air was filled with the sweet scent of pine and the soft rustle of leaves. As he walked through this tranquil setting, he heard the faint, rapid thumping of feet against the forest floor. Curiosity piqued, he followed the sound until he came upon a small clearing.

There, a nimble rabbit darted between the trees, its ears perked and eyes wide with fear. The rabbit was tempting, and he felt excitement and an urge to pounce. He remembered Schem when she taught him to control his mind to help him jump into the cold water. With that reminder, he quickly regained his thoughts. His plan being fixed on the target he again remembered, but now it was Heepah's advice, to become the hunter. And the hunter is patient. So, he waited and observed the rabbit. "I don't want to lose her in the brush," he thought. And he positioned himself to attack in front of the rabbit's fortress. And at the right moment, the attack was on. The rabbit zigzagged through the trees, seeking any path to freedom, but the coyote was relentless, every muscle in its body coiled and ready to pounce.

The rabbit, desperate and quick, veered sharply to the left, attempting to lose the coyote in a dense thicket. But the coyote was cunning and agile, effortlessly navigating the tangled foliage. Pelon could feel the tension rising, every second stretching out, as the chase neared its climax.

The rabbit, sensing its pursuer closing in, made a final, desperate sprint across an open patch of ground. The coyote, seeing its chance, gathered its strength and lunged forward, jaws open and ready to seize its prey. Just as the coyote's teeth were about to close around the rabbit, Pelon jolted awake, a gasp escaping his lips.

His surroundings came into sharp focus: the dimly lit tent, the muted sounds of the night, and the distant murmur of the hills settling into slumber. Pelon took a moment to steady his breathing, the vivid images of the dream still dancing behind his eyelids.

He rubbed his eyes and sat up, the adrenaline from the dream slowly ebbing away. The sense of urgency and impending danger lingered, a reminder of the real-life stakes that lay ahead. "A sign, perhaps," he mused to himself, "that the prize is there for me to grab."

Pelon knew he had to remain vigilant, both in his waking hours and in his dreams. The night held many secrets, and the dawn would bring new challenges. He will now head toward the confederate camp and cause their death.

The elders had taught him stories which appear fantastic at first but come to live with the night sky. Pelon looked at the moon and the stars and he could estimate that there were at least two more hours until dawn. *Thank you, old and wise ones*, he thought. There is plenty of time for him to sneak up on the bandidos. As he quietly made his way toward the Confederate camp, he could think about the two best ways to approach the attack. After a short internal debate, Pelon chose to be the hunter and to look for weakness.

The Confederates were still sleeping around a dying fire. Activity started in the camp at the crack of dawn, with a few cigarettes being lit. After that, the bandidos took their turns waking up and urinating. There was some excitement in the group as the men began fraternizing and laughing. They had a quick huddle, and two men grabbed their horses and rode quickly toward the mine. The remaining Confederates cleared out the camp and moved rocks to block the arroyo road. The count was still ten. Pelon now understood the plan, and he was ready to act.

Thwarted Ambush

Pelon made a hasty run toward the two bandidos. He had to catch up to them before they reached the caravan. It was his expectation to find the two hidden behind big boulders. Their job was not to start the attack, but it was to flank the convoy. He followed the tracks as the horses galloped, and then he stopped after the tracks showed the horses walking. *They are near,* he thought. Pelon no longer had the shadows to hide in. The bandidos are the ones in hiding somewhere nearby and a different approach is required.

He had to think quickly. He stashed his bow, arrows and his six shooter. And only kept a small flask. Pelon began laughing and swerving as he followed the trail. He was loud, hoping to call for attention. "Hay! Hay! Hay-hay! Canta y no llores!" Pelon sang. He soon reached the two bandidos, who took amusement at the drunken Indian. Pelon approached the first bandido, opened his hand and asked "Tequila?"

"Quiere tequila el pinche Indio!" they said in Spanish and burst in laughter.

Pelon laughed with them, tripping as he kept approaching them.

"Ta' loco el pinche Indio!" one said. Pelon was now an arm's length from one of the bandidos. He signaled for them to pay attention; they both did. He grabbed the snakehead from his waistband and made rattling sounds with his mouth. Then he turned the snake head to his face and pretended he was fighting it off. He turned, bumped onto one horse, turned again, struggling with the snake. He bumped into the other horse, showing a real struggle. Again, the bandidos found this amusing.

He then quickly slid the snakeskin from his waistband and threw it in front of one of the horses. The horse quickly rears and throws the bandido off. Pelon appears from under the rearing horse and sticks the snake's fangs on the second bandido's thigh and then pulls him off the saddle. The first bandido was laying down, grunting. He had landed on rocks and was in pain. The second bandido was making too much noise, so Pelon pistol whipped him with his own gun. They were hogtied, and Pelon took their horses.

Pelon grabbed his gear and raced toward the convoy. Once he reached the convoy, he went straight to James and clubbed him in the head. James' lifeless body slid head first on the right side of his saddle and hit the ground. The volunteers were surprised and confused. Pelon looked at one of the volunteers and said in Spanish, "Ve por Chato." The volunteer guard looked around and one of the old drivers moved his faced back toward the mine as an approval. And so, he went.

The mine was less than three miles away, but Chato and his guards were already on route. He joined them within minutes. "Un Indio mato a James!" said the rider. The guard revealed that James had been killed, and Chato replied that he was glad he hadn't wasted his lead. "En hora Buena! Ansina yo no gasto mi plomo! Vamonos! Jijos de la Chingada!" said Chato and they raced to the wagons.

The situation remained tense around the wagons. The volunteer guards felt relief that Chato was on his way, they trust-ed him to sort things out. And they maintained their eyes set on Pelon, who remained stoic on the horse. Chato arrived and Pelon filled him in on the trap set by the Confederates. Tensioned turned to relief as it was now known that Pelon was on their side. They planned on Pelon going ahead of the party to flank the bandidos and that Chato and his guards would ad-vance afterwards. The wagons and their mule teams would wait.

The Confederate spies had underestimated the resolve and preparedness of Burke's men. Pelon circled the hill on a game trail opposite of where the trap was being laid, left the horse and climbed the peak. He could hear their conversations as he got closer. It was the Southern drawl he had heard talking with James a few nights ago. The barricade was laid out to completely stop the convoy as they follow the dry wash. The remaining bandidos took cover around the trails while the four Confederates remained at the rear of the trap. Each Confederate pointed a long rifle at the trail.

Pelon had his bow and arrows in hand; he did not use a quiver. Crouched behind rocks, he had a clear line of sight to the four Confederates. He stuck three arrows on the ground and loaded his fourth. Pelon was out of breath, barely able to

hold his bow straight, he remembered Schem, "...When you learn to control your breath and calm your heart, you're not just preparing for cold water; you're learning to quiet the storm inside. You will let your mind take over." With that memory he took a deep breath and as he exhaled, his mind began to focus.

He shot one, two, three and four. The arrows stuck like a pin on a cushion before the soldiers realized what was going on. *They will not walk out of here,* Pelon thought.

He made a quick dash down the hill. Two of the Confederates got up and walked towards their camp. They were arrow number one and number two, which were placed in the back and shoulder. Arrow number three hit a thorax, and the man laid there gasping for air before he died. The fourth arrow hit the Confederate in the belly. As Pelon neared, this one sat there with one hand on his wound and the other reached for his gun. He got a shot at Pelon, which he evaded. Pelon didn't slow down and used his club to knock the gun out of his hand and then bashed in the soldier's face with a swing.

The two Confederates that were still mobile had dropped their rifles and attempted to escape, stumbling through the smooth river rocks. "These will be my singing birds," Pelon thought. He tripped them and disarmed them once on the ground. After taking their guns, he took his club to their feet. Pelon then plucked his arrows and disappeared. The Confederates cry out in agony.

The bandidos were calling out to the Confederates. They had heard the gunshot but were not able to see what went on. "Hawk," they would yell.

Chato, his men and the volunteer guards arrived, and that added to the bandido's confusion. The two smarter ones saw the numbers and calculated the shift in control. They fled. The remaining two soon followed. Chato's men went after them.

Pelon reappeared when Chato gained control. "I got the Confederates. The runners, they were here for a good time, not a long time. They will not be worth your chase."

"Orale!" said Chato. He yelled at his men, followed by a loud whistle. "Vengan muchachos! Dejen que se vayan a la Chingada!" Chato waved them to come back.

As the dust settled, the spies lay defeated, their plan thwarted. Pelon remained stoic, but took a moment to ponder the situation as the weight of the moment was sinking in. The convoy was safe, for now.

Turning to Chato, Pelon pointed at the two remaining Confederates. "Chiquititos, estos van hablar como un loro!" Chato said with a happy expression.

Chato's men cleared the barricade. He had two men make a dash back to the mine for a light wagon. They will take the two Confederates back on the buggy and keep them alive for interrogation. Chato had two of his guards remain with the caravan along with the volunteer guards until Poston's men joined.

As the convoy continued its journey, Pelon knew that the battle was far from over. The threat of espionage and theft would persist, but with Chato and his loyal team by his side, Pelon was prepared to confront whatever challenges lay ahead. He picked up his gear, saddled Ruby, and set out to follow the convoy. The protection of Paddy's interests was paramount, and Pelon would stop at nothing to ensure their safety.

The sun beat down on the dusty trail as the convoy rattled and creaked beneath their heavy cargo. Copper and lead ingots, bound for the smelters in Pittsburg, weighed down the vehicles, making every bump and jolt a potential threat to the precious cargo. As they approached Painted Rock, the convoy's tension grew. An escort signaled the drivers to slow down, as they had spotted a group of about six men waiting under the shade of a mesquite. One of the guards rode ahead to talk with the men. It appeared to be a friendly exchange; he rode back saying it was Poston's men. Everyone was relieved that the additional security had arrived. The convoy continued without further incidents, riding day and night, and successfully made it to the Glamis station the next day.

Pelon continued to work in the background, nowhere to be seen, but anticipated any point for an ambush and kept an eye for suspicious behavior. Once the metals were loaded, Pelon rode back to the Yuma rancheria and got some well-deserved rest. He met with Paddy the following week to debrief. When they met, Paddy expressed how proud he was of Pelon, when they locked arms, he looked Pelon in the eyes. "I'm so glad to see you in good health, my lad, after what you've been through."

Poston continued his fruitful relationship with President Lincoln. In March 1863, the president appointed him Superintendent of Indian Affairs. Paddy, meanwhile, continued as a special agent for the Union's mining operations in Arizona-New Mexico Territory.

One evening, as they sat on the porch watching the stars twinkle to life, Poston turned to Burke and said, "You know, my friend, I think we've made a real difference. The Union's going to win this war, and we've played a small part in it."

Paddy smiled, his eyes shining with pride. "We've done more than that, Charles. We've shown that even in the most remote corner of the country, patriotism, ingenuity, and loyalty can make a real impact."

As the night wore on, the two friends clinked their cups together in a toast to the Union, to their friendship, and to the copper that had brought them together in this wild and beautiful desert landscape.

By 1863, the Arizona Territory separated from New Mexico, and the war raged on in the East. Poston and Burke continued to work tirelessly, expanding their mining operation and supplying the Union with critical resources, for the fight in the West continued to be of supplies. They faced challenges, of course — Apache raids, equipment failures, and the ever-present threat of Confederate sympathizers. But through it all, the cunning and bravery of Pelon always assured their success.

Pigeon

Pigeon's childhood was loaded with struggles and solitude. As one of the many orphans, he faced frequent disdain and dismissal without a family to call his own. While the local community was close-knit, it often overlooked these children, and by thoughtful design disguised as compassion, found themselves in Christian missions. There, the first thing done was the shearing of their hair, followed by instilling a fear in them — a fear of their own thoughts, of an entity known as the devil, and of death itself. They were taught that their ancestral ways were evil, and they now belonged to a strict deity, one that was detached from the natural world and day-to-day survival. Pigeon fought against every effort to be included in the mission, ultimately having to take care of himself. Navigating between the town streets and the riverbank, he became adept at depending on his own cleverness and tenacity to survive.

One fateful day, as Pigeon played sticks with other kids, he encountered Pelon, a revered elder known for his wisdom and past exploits. Pelon's eyes, warm with compassion, saw beyond the young man's rugged exterior to the deep well of pain within, much like his own childhood. Pelon knew Pigeon had no home or family. But, as he walked, pretended to ignore Pigeon. There was a connection and they both knew it. Pigeon didn't talk much and in fact never even said hello but followed Pelon. It was time for Pigeon to leave the games behind and start learning a trade.

Pigeon preferred to hunt for rabbits with Pelon. But they also filled baskets with mesquite flour, one of the most precious and nutritious foods in the desert. This was a tradition practiced in the summer. The mesquite tree, with its feathery leaves and yellow flowers, was a gift from the creator spirit. It provided shade, firewood, medicine, and food. The pods that grew on its branches were sweet and crunchy when fresh and was dried and ground into flour for making breads and cakes.

Pigeon loved the mesquite pods. He would collect them from the ground or climb the trees to shake them off the branches. He would fill his baskets with as many pods as he could carry and take them to the communal grinding stone.

There, he would join other men and women who pounded the pods with stone pestles, breaking them into smaller pieces. Then, they would sift the pieces through baskets or cloths, separating the seeds from the husks. The seeds were then ground again, finer and finer, until they became a fine powder. This was the mesquite flour, which was stored for later use.

But the mesquite flour was not ready to eat yet. It had a bitter taste that had to be removed by rinsing. Pigeon learned this from Pelon, who showed him a trick. He took some flour and mixed it with water in a large pot. Pelon used warm water and a pinch of lime, and if done correctly, the flour would be ready with one rinse. If the water is too hot, the flour would be ruined.

He then poured the mixture through a cloth in a basket, letting the water drain out. Most folks repeated this process several times, until the water came out clear and the flour lost its bitterness. The rinsed flour was then spread on a cloth or mat to dry in the sun. When it was dry, it was ready to be cooked into delicious dishes.

Under Pelon's guidance, Pigeon discovered a sense of belonging he had never known. The elder's generosity and patience helped deal with the wounds of his past, and Pigeon's ability to track animals began to blossom. He learned the ancient traditions of his people, the intricacies of navigating the new white man's world, and the delicate balance of the desert ecosystem.

As the spring sun rose over the Yuma valley, a frail and struggling foal was born on a family farm. Its legs were twisted at awkward angles, indicating a clear defect. The weary owners, worn from years of hard work, looked upon the weak creature with a mix of sadness and pragmatism.

"It's mercy to put it down now," the owner said, his voice firm but tinged with regret. Pigeon typically withheld emotions, but this time showed compassion and pleaded for the foal's life. "Please, Lechero, don't take his life! I'll care for it and nurse it back to health!"

Lechero raised an eyebrow, skeptical. "You think you can save it? It's a lost cause, boy."

Pigeon's eyes shone with determination. "I'll try, Lechero! I'll do everything in my power!"

Reluctantly, Lechero unloaded his gun. "If I give you this horse, it's your responsibility. You're accountable for its life and its death. If it don't get better, you'll put it down yourself." Pigeon nodded fervently as Lechero handed him a bullet. "It's your duty now. Show it kindness but don't let it suffer." Fighting back tears, Pigeon pocketed the bullet.

As Lechero walked away, Pigeon cradled the foal in his arms, whispering words of comfort. He named the horse Risueño due to its odd blowing sound. Believing it would fare better with its mother, Pigeon stayed by their side. Before the day ended, he sought help from Pelon, who agreed but cautioned that sometimes nature must take its course.

From Pigeon's description, Pelon devised a plan. He instructed Pigeon to fetch fresh milk and found an old leather glove. They poured the milk into a glass flask, fitting the glove over the opening to mimic a teat. Returning to Risueño, they discovered the foal nearly lifeless but able to feed. Pigeon fed and cared for it diligently through long nights. Slowly and miraculously, Risueño began to thrive. Its legs straightened, its coat shone, and its spirit soared.

Pigeon's dedication revived the sickly horse, forging an unbreakable bond between them. While Pigeon grew into a strong and capable young man, the scars of his past no longer defined him. Instead, he found a sense of purpose with Risueño and a sense of belonging with Pelon.

Although Pigeon and Pelon were inseparable, Pelon's bouts with alcohol occasionally caused him to push Pigeon away. He didn't want Pigeon to witness his lows and ordered him to keep his distance. Time seemed to stand still for Pigeon during Pelon's absences, which sometimes lasted days or even weeks. Yet each time, Pelon returned, and their bond resumed as before.

Creation Story

Early that summer, as they rested under the shade of a mesquite tree, Pelon decided to share with Pigeon the story of their origin. He spoke in a gentle but authoritative voice, as if he had witnessed the events himself.

In their dialect, he asked, "Pigeon, do you know where we came from? Do you know why we live by the river?" Pelon didn't really wait for an answer, he smiled and continued, "Well, let me tell you then. It is a story that every *Quechan* should know and remember, for it is the story of our people and our land. Listen carefully, for this is how it happened."

Pigeon was familiar with the creation story, but he enjoyed Pelon's version.

"Long ago, before there were any humans on earth, there were only the Creator and an old man, who lived in the water. The Creator decided to make space and then found it to be lonely and boring, so they decided to make our world a live and special one. The old man had gone blind during the creation, and when he took some clay from the earth to make its inhabitants, they came out with webbed hands and feet. The Creator didn't approve of these and kicked them into the water. They became the creatures of the river. The old man went in after them but was not able to bring them to the surface. He created a whirlpool where sickness, pestilence and plague came out of. The Creator tried to stop it by placing his foot in the whirlpool but was not able to.

"The Creator continued with his work, making everything we see in the sky and grabbed mud and molded it into different shapes. He made birds and beasts, fish and reptiles, plants and insects. The Creator then breathed life into them and gave them names. He placed them all over the earth, in the mountains and valleys, in the forests and deserts, in the oceans and lakes. He was pleased with the work but still felt something was missing.

"The Creator wanted to make a creature that was different from the rest, a creature that could rule over the other creatures, one that could think and ask questions. So, he took some more clay and made a man and a woman. They were the people, called the *Quechan*. Then the Creator took them and gave them intelligence and free will, and he taught them how to speak and pray. He told them to multiply and fill the earth, and to take care of the other creatures. Just like they made fish for the water, birds for the air and rabbits for the land, they made desert people, mountain people and coastal people. We were first made as desert people, able to endure the harsh conditions and find food and water where others could not. We were placed in a fertile valley, where we built a village and stayed every season. He was happy with his creation, and he blessed them with generations."

"For many years, our people lived in peace and harmony with the spirit and the other creatures. They were grateful for the gifts they had received, and they praised the spirit every day. They were happy and prosperous, and they had many children. The valley was their home, and they loved it."

"But one day, everything changed. A great drought came upon the land, and the sun burned hotter than ever. The crops withered and died, and the animals fled. The water sources dried up, and our people became thirsty and hungry. They prayed to the Creator spirit for help, but he did not answer. They wondered if he had abandoned them, or if he was angry with them. They grew desperate and fearful, and some of them lost their faith. Those that endured became resourceful and hardened by their experience.

"The Creator spirit saw their plight, and he felt sorry for them. He had not abandoned them, nor was he angry with them. He had simply been busy with other things, and he had gone tired from the creation efforts. He had not noticed the drought. He decided to do something to help them. He took his staff and struck the earth with it, making a deep crack that crossed valleys and mountains so far that you can follow it for months and not see its end. From the crack, water gushed out, forming a stream that flowed through all the features. The stream became a river, and the river, by the time it reached our land, it is wide and beautiful. The land became green again, and the crops grew back. The animals returned, and our people had food and water again. They rejoiced and thanked the Creator spirit for his gift."

"The Creator spirit told them that he had made them river people now, and that they had to live by the river and take care of it. He told them that the river was their lifeblood, and that they had to protect it from harm. 'You will thrive,' the spirit told them. He emphasized that the other creatures that lived by the river were their brothers, and that they had to treat them well. He added that the other people that lived in the deserts, the mountains and the coast were their cousins, and that they had to trade with them and help them. He told them that he loved them all, and that he would always watch over them."

"That is how we became river people," Pelon concluded. "That is why we respect the spirit, and why we honor our ancestors. That is why we are the people (*Quechan*), and why we are proud of it."

Pigeon listened to the story with awe and wonder. He felt pride. He looked at Pelon with admiration and affection, and he felt a bond between them that was stronger than blood. He realized that he was his family, his people, and his home. More importantly, Pigeon found purpose.

Constables

Nestled by the Colorado River, Yuma's wild desert landscape attracted pioneers, miners and traders, making it both beautiful and dangerous. By 1874, Arizona City was now Yuma and it began to grow rapidly with settlers, miners, and even outlaws. To maintain order, the county established a constable position. O.F. Townsend was appointed as its first constable.

Townsend, a rugged and just individual, took his oath seriously. He patrolled the dusty streets diligently, maintaining peace and enforcing territorial laws. During his tenure, he notably confronted the notorious outlaw "Curly Bill" Brocius, convincing him to leave town without incident.

A stern and principled man, Townsend was tasked with imposing law and order where the concept was fledgling. Armed with no more than a revolver and a badge, his duty extended beyond apprehending wrongdoers; he also mediated disputes, protected settlers, and fostered a community based on respect and the rule of law.

With keen eyes and a quick draw, Townsend soon earned the townspeople's respect. Known for his fairness and measured approach to conflict resolution, under his watch Yuma began to transform from a lawless settlement into a community where residents could securely build their lives.

Over the course of twelve years, Yuma experienced steady growth. In 1886, Will Smith assumed the position of constable. With prior experience in nearby mining towns, Smith brought a seasoned and practical approach to law enforcement in Yuma, addressing issues that ranged from saloon fights to cattle theft.

An example from Smith's service includes resolving a heated conflict between rival mining corporations. By stepping in and defusing the tension, he prevented any potential violence, earning the community's admiration for his composed handling of the situation.

As Yuma expanded, there was a growing demand for a more formalized law enforcement presence. That same year, Will Smith took on the full role of constable. A man of decisive action, Smith possessed a military background that had equipped him well for frontier challenges. His more direct and assertive methods contrasted with Townsend's but were precisely what Yuma required at that time.

During Smith's tenure, Yuma's borders extended, and its population increased, bringing with it a rise in problems such as land disputes, cattle rustling, and occasional robberies. Smith confronted these challenges vigorously, organizing a posse to track down criminals and collaborating closely with adjacent towns to limit the outlaws' refuge options.

One of Smith's notable successes was his capture of the infamous bandit "Black Jack" Ketchum. Through persistent pursuit and strategic planning, Smith managed to bring the outlaw to justice, further solidifying his reputation as an exceptional lawman. His efforts played a significant role in enhancing safety for the residents of Yuma.

In the year 1887, T.D. Lockwood assumed the role of constable. Lockwood's period in office was characterized by heightened tensions between settlers and Native American tribes. He collaborated closely with Sheriff John "Jack" McCullough to maintain peace and address conflicts.

During his tenure, a group of Quechan Indians opposed the nearby railway construction. Lockwood and McCullough engaged with the tribe, addressing their concerns and achieving a peaceful resolution.

Known for his progressive vision, Lockwood understood that Yuma needed more than just enforcement; it required organization and modernization. He aimed at forming a formal police force, incorporating adequate training and protocols. New investigative techniques and record-keeping practices were introduced under his direction, enhancing the efficiency of law enforcement. Lockwood also promoted community engagement, believing that a strong rapport between law enforcement and the community was essential for peace.

During Lockwood's leadership, Yuma established its first jailhouse and an elementary court system. These institutions played a crucial role in providing justice and accountability to the town. His forward-looking approach set the foundation for a more organized and effective law enforcement framework in Yuma.

In 1888, Frank Burke was appointed as Yuma's constable. As a respected community leader, Burke dedicated himself to reducing crime and fostering strong relationships with local businesses, ultimately contributing to Yuma's growth as a bustling commercial hub. Frank stood six feet tall and was noted for his calm and courage; he was never known to be afraid of anything. He had seen his share of violence and bloodshed, but he never lost his sense of justice or compassion.

As a justice of the peace, Burke was responsible for managing legal affairs and ensuring justice in a town where conflicts occurred frequently. His experience in hand-to-hand combat and professional boxing added to his authoritative presence, but his measured approach and commitment to justice defined his role. Burke never backed down from danger and approached each case with careful consideration.

His tenure also saw him implement work programs for inmates at the Yuma Territorial Prison, allowing prisoners to contribute to the community while spending time outside the prison walls. Burke was well-liked and became deputy sheriff of Yuma Couty in 1889.

On a Monday afternoon, January 13, 1890, shortly after the arrival of the westbound train, the sheriff's office received reports that John Sevenoaks was intoxicated and brandishing a revolver around town. Burke located Sevenoaks and demanded he surrender the weapon. Denying possession, Sevenoaks eventually pulled out the gun while verbally abusing Burke. Swiftly reacting, Burke turned, cocked his revolver, and ordered Sevenoaks to raise his hands. After some hesitation, Sevenoaks complied, and Burke disarmed and arrested him, taking him to the county jail.

The following Friday, Under Sheriff Mayes was escorting prisoner John Sevenoaks from jail to the courtroom when William Johnson, another inmate, escaped. Within an hour, then Deputy Sheriff Burke had recaptured Johnson two miles west of town. Charged with breaking into a railroad car and stealing shoes, Johnson was being held in custody pending his appearance before the Grand Jury because he failed to post bail. Burke felt compassion for Johnson and offered to help him with the bail. But Johnson was sour about his capture and didn't agree to the proposal.

At the subsequent hearing, Judge Ira Mabbett set Sevenoaks' bail at $400 for his Grand Jury appearance. He posted bail and was released. Burke earned a significant commendation for his composed and decisive actions, which likely prevented harm to all involved.

Despite the inherent dangers, Burke joined the posse pursuing the criminals, driven by his dedication to the law. This pursuit represented more than just capturing outlaws; it underscored Yuma's strong stance on justice and its intolerance for lawlessness.

The early constables of Yuma — O.F. Townsend, Will Smith, T.D. Lockwood, and Frank Burke — each played a pivotal role in shaping the town's identity. Their efforts transformed Yuma from a chaotic frontier settlement into a community where law and order prevailed.

Townsend's establishment of a foundation for justice, Smith's relentless pursuit of outlaws, Lockwood's modernization of law enforcement, and Burke's dedication to fairness and integrity, all contributed to the town's growth and stability. These men were more than just lawmen; they were the pillars upon which Yuma was built.

Their legacy lives on in the streets of Yuma, in the stories passed down through generations, and in the continued efforts of those who strive to uphold the principles of justice and community that they championed. The early constables of Yuma were the guardians of the wild frontier, and their impact on the town is a testament to their courage, vision, and unwavering commitment to the rule of law.

Looking for Pelon

Last Sunday night, just a few steps from the ferry dock, the group enjoyed a substantial meal before setting off to find Pelon. This area used to be known as Jaeger City, until it was devastated by the flood of 1862. One of the buildings served as the Fort Yuma Mail station, operated by the Butterfield Overland Mail Company. The location once boasted a small urban hub by the river with a pleasant hotel, two blacksmiths, a livery stable, two general stores, and several residences. Most people came here for business dealings with travelers. Now, everything has been swept away, leaving only reed huts similar to those built by the native inhabitants.

That evening was still very pleasant when it comes to the weather, although the night was expected to progress on the cooler side. The night's fires seemed louder than usual, with howling and staggering pandemonium of bestialized men. Men moved about, in obvious intoxication, swerving from side to side much as river reeds on a windy day. The night was not a quiet one, as it is laden with drunken attempts in song, filthy language and drunken laughter. There were those that attempted conversation, yet most were too drunk to articulate.

An unknown man stopped the group and began telling drunken jokes. These must have been funny, seeing he continued to laugh hysterically as the group walked away. We looked around at each other's face and all with question marks. A group of men was now heading to the ferry. It is possible that they have finished their activities and are returning home across the river, but it is more likely that they will continue seeking whiskey. Frank knew most of these faces, not more than 20 years past they were proud braves aiming to push back at the settlers who would not respect property lines and who's livestock often ruined crops. But their bravery was not enough and all Colorado River tribes were eventually subdued and have not since made hostile demonstrations.

The Indian agents had some involvement in the appeasement of the brave with the promises of abundant food, property, and other goods. The Indian wars eventually died down, and that is exactly when the promises of the Indian agents were proven empty. Hungry and lost in their way some have stolen food while some have turned to bigger crimes. Those that have turned to the drink have even taken life, in the numbers similar to the drunken white men.

Frank should find Pelon amongst the drunken horde, drowning the memories of his restless youth, longing for the river life he grew up with. Or he could be selling whiskey, as complaints of this sort had been made in '85. His people survived encounters with the Spanish and the pelt traders, and he recounts these events. Pelon hung on to the memory of the great Chief Palma and his successful scrimmages against the invading forces. Pelon was one of those braves. He was also a survivor of the Maricopa Wells ambush that decimated the braves' numbers.

Never subdued, the Yuma maintained their aboriginal culture mostly unchanged until the Indian wars arrived at their doorsteps. From 1848 to 1852, the Yuma fought off western disease, scalp hunters, and the American Army, and for it paid a hefty price. During that timeframe, the community went from a population of about 3,000 down to 972.

Frank and his companions looked around but hadn't located Pelon. He will have to put the word out that he was looking for him and had in hand a good-paying contract to track a criminal. "If you see Pelon, tell him Frank Burke is looking for him."

Frank recalled how they had teamed up in the past, and how he had known Pelon since childhood. Pelon had been good friends with Frank's father, Paddy, and together they had caught some outlaws in their time. Pelon hadn't been doing so well since Paddy died. Pelon was at his best when he was on the trail. The west didn't know of a better scout. He didn't drink a sip of the fire water while tracking either. Frank noted one strange idiosyncrasy; Pelon spent as much time observing the sky as he did observing the ground. To Frank, it seemed unnecessary, since the criminal they were after was ground-bound and hadn't taken flight like a bird. Even when people said, "he took flight," they didn't mean it literally. But, given Pelon's effectiveness, Frank intended to allow him to gaze at the stars until he reached satisfaction and without interruption.

Hopefully, Frank's word finds him well. Last he heard of Pelon, the man had gotten into a drunken altercation with Jim, another Yuma. Jim walked away with shallow knife cuts to his face and arms, but Pelon's head found the blunt end of a club. While the medicine man attended to their wounds, the conversation in town was about the whiskey and how these men may have been furnished with such spirits. It so happens that the white folk wanted to have their drink but found the Indians undeserving. Such logic had always fascinated Frank.

Pelon is Found

That afternoon was hot and dusty when Frank saw Pigeon walk into the sheriff's office. He had a dirty bandana around his neck and a hat too big on his head. He looked like he had been traveling for days, but he didn't say a word. He just nodded at Frank and motioned with his hand to follow. Frank knew Pigeon was one of Pelon's friends and assumed he had some information about Pelon's location.

Frank grabbed his hat and followed Pigeon out of the office. They mounted their horses and rode out of town, heading east.

Pigeon's horse was a sorry sight. He was smaller than most, and his coat was patchy and dull. His ears were long and floppy, and his tail was thin and ragged. He looked like a wet dog that had been left out in the sun. But he had one thing that made him stand out from the rest — his blowing. Whenever Pigeon stopped him or urged him on, the horse would blow through his nostrils in a peculiar way. He would blow three times in a row. It almost sounded like he was laughing at something or mocking people. Maybe he knew something the people didn't. Maybe he thought this whole thing was a joke. Frank didn't know what to make of it, but it sure annoyed him.

Pigeon didn't seem to mind. He patted his horse and whispered in its ear, as if they shared a secret. Frank wondered what kind of bond they had, and how they had met. He wondered if Pigeon's horse was as loyal as he was, or if it would run away at the first sign of trouble.

Frank followed Pigeon and kept up with him. Pigeon didn't speak or look back, but Frank had no choice but to trust him.

Pigeon had been a troublemaker in the past, caught stealing food and fighting. But now he was known for his loyalty to Pelon.

Maybe he had heard about the contract and wanted to join us, young kids are always out to prove themselves. Or maybe he had some trouble of his own and needed our help. Either way, Frank was curious to see what Pigeon had to show him.

They rode for about half an hour, crossing fields and dry creeks, until they reached the Gila at a point where it flowed through a grove of mesquite trees, deep in the Dome Valley. The completeness of the trail would be underwater most of the year, so most people stayed away. Pigeon slowed and pointed to a spot under the shade of a large tree. There, Frank saw Pelon lying on a blanket, snoring loudly. He had a bottle of whiskey in his hand and a pile of empty ones around him. Pelon looked like he had been there for a while, drinking himself into oblivion.

Pigeon dismounted and walked over to Pelon. He kicked him gently in the ribs and said something in Quechan Language.

Pelon stirred and opened his eyes. He blinked and looked at Pigeon, then said "nyaa'aly," and rolled to his side, "...a'aly." Pigeon kicked him again, and Pelon was agitated but before asking Pigeon to leave him alone, he saw Frank. He worked up a smile and tried to get up, but he was too drunk to stand. He slurred something and laughed, then fell back on his rear.

Late summers in Yuma are as hot as the devil's crotch. Frank had to get out of the sun so he dismounted and joined them under the tree. Frank looked at Pelon and shook his head. He was a mess, and Frank wondered if he was fit for the job. He said, "Pelon, I'm glad to see you alive, but you're in no shape to track a criminal. We have a contract to catch the train robbers, and we need to leave soon. Can you sober up and join us?"

Pelon looked at Frank and nodded. "Frank, I could smell you a mile away. You smell just like your father, only more stubborn. Can you sit by me for a minute?"

Frank squatted on the ground next to Pelon and listened attentively.

"I had a dream that I was drowning, and Pigeon couldn't help me. In this dream I seek the wisdom of the spirit, and somehow end up in the water before I can reach him. The thought of being lost to the spirit scares me and I find relief in the drink. And then I fall asleep again and seek to get close to the spirit again. And I drown again."

Pelon looked at the sky and said a few words in his language. As he described his dream, he was thinking of its meaning and how it relates to Frank. Pelon had always been a tracker, a hunter, a man of the land. He had followed the spirit's guidance and found his way in the wilderness. He had faced many dangers and challenges, but he had never feared death. And he was honorable, the only man Frank's father trusted with his life. Pelon had always good faith in the spirit to show him the right path. But now, he felt lost. He was awake and maybe he was drowning in a sea of confusion; what else can Frank understand from his dream? Maybe Pelon felt abandoned by the spirit, or worse, rejected. He felt like he had no purpose, no reason to live.

Pelon looked at Frank, and a surge of relief came upon him. Frank had been his friend for many years and his father before that was a loyal partner and a brave companion. Frank had seen him at his best and his worst and had never judged him. Frank had always respected Pelon and his ways, even when they were different from his own. Frank had come to him with an offer, an invitation, a challenge. Frank asked him to join him in a manhunt, to track down some outlaws who had robbed a train and killed people. They needed his skills, his experience, his wisdom. Frank give him a chance to redeem himself, to prove himself, to find himself again.

Pelon felt a spark of hope in his heart. He realized that this was what he needed, what he wanted. He needed to go on a journey, a quest, a pilgrimage. He needed to face a new challenge, a new enemy, a new land. He needed to seek the spirit in a different way, in a different place, in a different form. He needed to renew his bond with nature, with life, with himself. He needed to find his balance, his peace, his joy. He needed to live again.

"I'm glad Pigeon went and got you. Many things are in my mind, but I'm ready now. Give me some water and some coffee, and I'll be fine." He handed Frank the bottle of whiskey and asked Frank to throw it away. Frank did as he asked and gave him some water from his canteen. He drank it and coughed. Pigeon had readied a fire and put some water on. Pelon said, "Thank you, Frank. You're a good man. And Pigeon should have left me here to die, but I guess this old Indian has grown on him."

Frank watched as Pelon and he shared a few cups of coffee in quiet. He looked at Pelon, noting how he had aged since they last rode together. Frank feared Pelon's better days might be behind him. However, he saw that Pelon had Pigeon with him and figured he must be passing down his knowledge. Frank thought this would be a great opportunity for that. It had been his experience that Pelon was a better man when he was trailing.

Pelon smiled and gestured toward the road. He said, "Let's go, Frank. Let's go and get them." He got up and stumbled, but Pigeon caught him and helped him onto his horse. He tapped Pigeon's hand with gratitude. Pigeon nodded and continued to his horse. He still didn't say a word, but he didn't need to.

They rode out of the muddy trail, following Pigeon. Back in Yuma, they would pick up provisions and catch the next train to Fresno.

They arrived at Yuma in the late afternoon, the sun would not be setting over the Colorado River for three more hours. The town began bustling with activity shortly after they arrived, as people are more active toward the evening and avoid the high sun heat. Goods moved along the streets and the railroad tracks. Yuma was a vital junction for the Southern Pacific Railroad, which had connected California to the rest of the country since 1878. From here, trains could go west to San Francisco, Los Angeles, or east to Tucson and beyond.

Frank and his companions bought their tickets for the next train to Fresno, scheduled to leave around midnight. As they waited, Pelon recounted the story of his first train ride, which had been with Frank's father. They had ridden horseback to the Glamis station, but the operator refused to let Pelon board the passenger coach, insisting that Indians had to ride in the cargo cars. The train's departure was delayed as Frank's father, Old Paddy, stood his ground, arguing that Pelon was a person, not baggage, and deserved a seat like anyone else. The operator eventually relented after a brief delay, realizing that the other passengers were beginning to support Paddy's stance.

Frank always enjoyed hearing this story, especially since Pelon had teasingly accused him of being the stubborn one earlier that day. The memory of Paddy's unwavering determination and the camaraderie between his father and Pelon brought a smile to Frank's face. They shared a deep bond, and Frank felt proud to continue the legacy of loyalty and friendship.

The Southern Pacific was popular and profitable, thanks to the vision and ambition of its owners, led by Collis Huntington. He and his partners had expanded their network by acquiring other railroads and building new lines across the Southwest. They had faced many challenges and rivals, such as the Texas and Pacific Railroad, which had planned to link El Paso to the Pacific Ocean. But Huntington had outsmarted them by reaching Deming, New Mexico, first and joining forces with the Santa Fe Railroad. This had created the second transcontinental route in the nation and secured the Southern Pacific's dominance in the region.

Frank and his companions spent the night waiting for the train, observing the people bustling in and out of the bars. They were weary and hungry after the long day and the ride from the grove. Although Pelon seemed to be feeling better, his weakness and pallor were still evident. Pigeon stayed by his side, while Frank wandered around the town, searching for a place to buy food and supplies.

He entered Gandolfo's, a small store that offered bread, cheese, and canned goods. Frank also bought a newspaper, hoping to find some information about the Collins train robbers.

Frank returned to the station and joined Pelon and Pigeon. They had dinner and Frank read the newspaper, scanning the headlines, looking for anything that might interest them.

There was an article at the bottom of the U.S. news section, about the Collins train robbery. It said that a detective named Will Smith had tracked down the robbers to a hideout near Fresno but had been ambushed and wounded by them. He had managed to escape, but the robbers had fled with the loot. The article criticized Smith's decision to go in after the bandits and not wait for a posse, which was en route.

Frank folded the newspaper and put it in his pocket. He looked at the clock and saw that it was almost midnight. They heard the whistle of a train, and wondered if it was their ride. Frank felt a surge of excitement. This is why Frank manhunts; it is a special rush.

Train Robbery

The moon cast a silver glow over the rolling hills of California's Central Valley. On Wednesday, August 3rd, 1892, and the Southern Pacific's Los Angeles night express train #17, departing from San Francisco, chugged steadily southward. The night express arrived at Collins station, a small, nondescript stop along the way and fifteen miles from Fresno. All going as planned, the train pulled out of Collins station, picking up speed. The train rattled rhythmically, lulling its passengers into a contemplative non-silence. The landscape outside shifted from the bustling town to quiet stretches of desert.

In the dark, four masked robbers, armed and poised, awaited their moment. They had been tracking the train's route for days, studying its schedule and cargo. Tonight was the night. As the train gained momentum, the robbers sprang into action. Suddenly, they mounted on swift horses and appeared from the darkness, racing alongside the train. They leaped aboard with ease, their intentions clear. Two boarded the engine, pistols drawn, while the others climbed into the express car.

About six miles past the station, the robbers made their way to the engine, and the engineer was forced to halt. The two robbers had him and the fireman covered with two double barrel shotguns. One of the bandits had with him dynamite and went out to the left side of the engine to the driving wheel piston. He placed a stick of dynamite and ordered the fireman to light the fuse.

Brandishing shotguns, they ordered the fireman to light the fuse on a stick of dynamite placed near the driving wheel piston. The dynamite was lit, and the explosion was horrific.

The explosion shattered the quiet night, breaking the piston rod and partially disabling the engine. The train jerked to a stop, and the passengers, rattled by the blast, began peeking out of their windows, only to be met with a hail of gunfire.

The passengers were rattled by the blast. Some put their heads out the windows, but their curiosity was met with a barrage of bullets and buckshot. At least two that formed this group were deputy sheriffs, and they were successfully neutralized by the firepower. The same with General Freight Agent Smurr, who reportedly offered no resistance.

The robbers ordered the engineer to get off the train and walk a short distance along the track, while they proceeded to light up the two doors of the express car by exploding dynamite cartridges, about eight detonations in all, which tore the doors into splinters and smashed the floor of the car. One passenger was seriously hurt by the blasts.

The masked robbers entered the express car, and covered Louis Roberts, the messenger, with their shotguns. The leader, a tall, imposing figure, barked orders. "Open the safe!" They ordered him to open the Wells, Fargo & Co's safe. Roberts set about doing this but was so excited he forgot the combination, and so informed the criminals. The thugs did not hold back and immediately struck him a heavy blow to the head with a pistol and followed with a threat to kill him if he did not open the safe immediately. This show of force helped the messenger recollect his thoughts and the combination to the safe. With trembling fingers, Roberts proceeded to open the safe. The safe door swung open, revealing stacks of cash, gold coins, and valuable securities. The bandits worked swiftly, filling sacks with loot.

Conductor William Davis, alerted to the robbery, sent a distress signal from the rear of the train. But the robbers were prepared. They had cut the telegraph wires ahead, ensuring no warnings would reach Fresno. Within minutes, the robbers vanished into the night, leaving behind a ransacked express car, shaken crew, train #17 in disrepair, and the passengers stranded.

Sheriff deputies and detectives scrambled to investigate. They tracked horse hoof prints and followed rumors, but the robbers seemed to have disappeared into the California darkness. This brazen robbery is bound to go down in history as one of the most audacious train heists of all time.

The time occupied in blowing open the car and securing the treasure was not more than 25 or 30 minutes. The authorities believed they took at least $50,000 from the messenger's safe.

The initial information on the assailants is scarce, two 5'9" to 5'11" tall men, 170lb, one of them sporting new overalls, and some other useless details about their hats and ware. Two more men were implicated, and more may have been involved, as evident by the gunfire that continued for the length of the hold up.

News of the audacious robbery rapidly spread far and wide. Due to the violent nature of the crime, the Dalton brothers were immediately considered prime suspects. Authorities from the Southern Pacific Railroad soon verified that the Daltons were in Idaho, far removed from California. The subsequent investigation ensued. Both Southern Pacific and Wells, Fargo & Co. promptly announced a $1,000 reward for any information leading to the apprehension of those involved in the heist.

The Way of the Bounties

Hunting for bounties was a risky and often unrewarding business in the 1890s. The rewards offered by the express companies, the railroads, and the government were contingent on the arrest and conviction of the outlaws, not their deaths. This meant that the bounty hunters had to capture the robbers alive, which was no easy feat considering the firepower and ferocity of the gangs they pursued.

The outlaws had an edge over the lawmen in several ways. They knew the terrain better, they had informants and sympathizers among the local population, and they could use any means necessary to escape or fight back. The bounty hunters, on the other hand, had to follow the rules of law and evidence, and avoid killing the outlaws unless absolutely necessary. They also had to deal with the competition and mistrust from other lawmen, who sometimes claimed the same rewards or tried to sabotage their efforts.

Many bounty hunters were former outlaws themselves, who turned to the other side of the law for various reasons. Some did it out of remorse, some out of desperation, and some out of greed. They were often despised by both the outlaws and the lawmen, who regarded them as traitors or mercenaries. They faced constant danger and uncertainty, and rarely received the recognition or respect they deserved. Some of them became famous, such as Pat Garrett, who killed Billy the Kid, or Charlie Siringo, who infiltrated the Wild Bunch. But many more died in obscurity or went back to their old ways of crime.

Charles L. Wilson captured two stage robbers sixteen years before, killing one of them. Mr. Wilson was only recently paid by Wells, Fargo & Co.'s Express the standing reward which he earned by capturing the second robber. He lost money by the shot he fired in defense of his own life, which killed the one robber.

"They don't offer rewards for deceased individuals," Mr. Wilson remarked. "This likely explains why the pursuit of Sontag and Evans hasn't been more aggressive. When hunting down such notorious criminals, there's always the risk of being ambushed or killed. Train robbers and stage robbers know what awaits them if they're caught, and they'll fight to the death if cornered. It's one thing to offer a reward for their capture, but if they're killed in the process, the person responsible gets nothing. Even the bravest individuals hesitate to take such risks under these conditions. You'll notice that the standing rewards are only for the arrest and conviction of robbers. I shot one in the hip when he resisted, and he died shortly after, so I received nothing for him. I have only just been paid $300 by Wells, Fargo & Co. for capturing his partner, Tom Brown. I'm still trying to claim a similar reward from the State of California and the United States, provided the statute of limitations doesn't expire."

In the end, the pursuit of outlaws like Sontag and Evans was as much a game of wits and endurance as it was one of firepower and violence. The line between the lawmen and the lawless blurred, as both sides played a deadly game of cat and mouse across the rugged terrain of the American West. The bounty hunters, navigated a treacherous path, risking their lives for uncertain rewards and the slim hope of redemption. The outlaws, knew that capture meant certain death or a life behind bars, and so they fought with the ferocity of cornered beasts.

As word of the Collins train robbery spread, the populace was gripped by a mixture of fear and fascination. Trains, the lifeblood of commerce and communication, had become the stage for dramatic confrontations that captured the imagination of the public. Sontag and Evans became infamous, their names spoken in hushed tones in saloons and around campfires. Stories of their daring exploits and narrow escapes became the stuff of legend, adding to the mystique of the American outlaw.

Yet, the relentless pursuit by detectives and deputies was making progress. The noose was tightening around Sontag and Evans, and their days of freedom were numbered. In the shadows of the Sierra Nevada Mountains, where they sought refuge and plotted their next move, the specter of justice loomed ever closer. The lawmen, armed with warrants and a dogged determination, were closing in, driven by the promise of reward and the pursuit of duty.

As dusk settled over the Californian landscape, the hunters and the hunted prepared for the final act in their deadly drama. The fate of Sontag and Evans hung in the balance, teetering on the edge of chaos and order, freedom and captivity. The West, with all its rugged beauty and untamed spirit, was the backdrop for this epic saga of crime and retribution, where legends were born and destinies were forged in the crucible of conflict.

The stage was set for a showdown that would echo through the annals of history, a testament to the enduring struggle between those who sought to uphold the law and those who dared to defy it. In this turbulent era, where heroes and villains often wore the same faces, the story of Sontag and Evans would serve as a poignant reminder of the harsh realities and fleeting glories of life on the edge of civilization.

Robbers Identified

On August 5, 1892, the Saturday after the Collins train was robbed, the streets of Visalia were covered with a reddish hue as the sun descended over the horizon. Two heavy wagons headed in opposite directions, each hurrying to get a last load across town before the sun went down. It had been two days since the audacious train robbery in Collins, and the town was still buzzing with the electrifying tale of the daring heist. As the lawmen pieced together the fragments of the crime, a lead emerged that would set in motion a series of events destined for infamy.

The atmosphere was thick with anticipation and unease, every whispered conversation weaving together a tapestry of speculation and intrigue. The robbery had not just been an attack on a train; it was a brazen challenge to the law and order, a gauntlet thrown down in the heart of the burgeoning West. The citizens of Visalia, with their roots sunk deep into the soil of frontier resilience, found their daily routines tinged with the excitement of imminent justice or further calamity.

Amidst this turbulent backdrop, the names of Sontag and Evans began to surface, whispered with both awe and trepidation. Their reputations preceded them — figures of both myth and menace, capable of acts that defied the imagination. And, in fact, they inspired sensationalism and a type of sympathy from many of the locals. The lawmen, armed with fresh clues and a renewed sense of purpose, knew that bringing these outlaws to justice would require more than just brawn and firepower; it would demand cunning, endurance, and a touch of the very audacity that their quarry so brazenly displayed.

Detectives Thacker and Hickey, alongside Sheriff Cunningham, had received credible information that painted a clear picture of the outlaws' movements. On the fateful Tuesday preceding the robbery, Chris Evans and John Sontag had hired a livery in Visalia, ostensibly to venture into the mountains. The significance of their journey became apparent when, just yesterday at noon, they returned with the horses' shoes conspicuously absent. The telltale signs pointed to a frantic escape into the rugged terrain, likely to conceal their ill-gotten gains.

Suspicion casts a long shadow over Sontag, who was no stranger to the watchful eyes of the law. His involvement in the Collins train robbery seemed all but certain, and the relentless pursuit by the detectives was now a race against time. The chase was on, and the lines between justice and vengeance blurred as the officers closed in on their quarry.

The scent of the hunt filled the air, and with every passing hour, the tension mounted. The rugged beauty of the Sierra Nevada mountains loomed in the distance, a stark reminder of the trials that lay ahead. For the detectives, this was more than a mission; it was a testament to their resolve and a fight for the very soul of the law. The saga of Chris Evans and John Sontag was at its beginning, and the echoes of their deeds would reverberate through history, a poignant reminder of the relentless pursuit of justice in the untamed West.

Collins, California, is a small town in the San Joaquin Valley, about 40 miles west of Fresno and 200 miles north of Los Angeles. It is located along the Southern Pacific Railroad line, which connected San Francisco and Sacramento with the southern part of the state. Collins was a farming community, surrounded by orchards and vineyards, and had a store, a hotel, a saloon, and a post office. It was the scene of the August 3rd daring and violent train robbery when John Sontag and Chris Evans stopped the express train and looted its contents.

John Sontag, a former railroad engineer, had been residing with Chris Evans. Chris Evans was a long-time resident of

Visalia and lived there with his wife and seven children. The two men met a year before the robbery at a livery stable in Modesto, which was eventually destroyed by a fire. They left their horses at the Modesto stable owned by Wilson, who also operated a nearby inn. They decided to stay at the inn for a few days.

During their stay, they rented rooms and spent most of their time in the saloon, drinking whiskey, playing cards, and interacting with the barmaids. Their friendship quickly developed, and they showed no inclination to leave anytime soon, resulting in a substantial bill at both the inn and the stable. However, their behavior soon sparked the curiosity and discontent of Wilson and his staff, who wondered how the men would settle their debts and were puzzled by their reckless conduct. Wilson also observed that one of the horses they had brought matched the description of a horse stolen from a ranch near Fresno. He decided to confront them about paying their bill and requested that they leave.

He found them in the saloon, surrounded by a crowd of drinking buddies. After approaching them politely, he handed them a paper with the amount they owed him. Sontag and Evans looked at the paper and laughed. They told Wilson that they had no intention of paying him, and that he should be grateful that they had chosen to patronize his establishment. They insulted him and mocked him, and then they drew their guns and threatened to kill him if he ever bothered them again.

Having worn their welcome, the pair decided to leave their celebration. That same night, the stable burned down, and they remained as the main suspects responsible for this fire.

John Sontag was a restless and reckless man who had a taste for adventure and danger. He had been a railroad engineer, but he quit his job after a serious accident that left him with a scarred face. He drifted from town to town, looking for opportunities to make quick money and have fun. He was fond of card games, horse races, and women, but he often got into trouble with the law or his rivals. He was not afraid of using violence or deception to get what he wanted, and he had a reputation as a skilled marksman and a daring outlaw. He joined forces with Chris Evans, an older and more experienced criminal, who became his mentor and partner in crime. He also fell in love with Evans' daughter, who admired his courage and charm. He hoped to marry her and settle down, but he could not resist the temptation of one last big robbery that would make him rich and famous.

Detective Will Smith took the lead in this investigation, so he made his way to Visalia to perform further inquiry. Detective Will Smith asked Deputy Sherif Witty to accompany him to Evans' house, in the north part of town, where, he stated,

he wanted to interview a man. They went to the house and found George Sontag, John Sontag's brother, and took him to jail for questioning. They returned to Evans' house and secured a trunk that supposedly contained the stolen coin.

While Deputy Sheriff Witty and Detective Smith were hitching their horses, they saw John Sontag enter the house. The officers asked a little girl in the house where Sontag was, and she said he was not in the house. Just then, Chris Evans entered the house through the back door. The house contained a sitting room, with a bedroom on the left side. In place of a door to the bedroom was a portiere. There was another bedroom next to the sitting room. Evans was in the latter bedroom. He said that Sontag had gone up to town. Smith told him that he had seen that Sontag enter the house. Smith stepped into the house and pulled aside the portiere, and there stood Sontag with a double-barrel shotgun. Smith stepped to one side and attempted to unbutton his coat to reach his six-shooter, when he saw that Chris Evans also had a shotgun.

Witty and Smith then ran out through the front door. Witty ran through the gateway and Smith went over the fence. Smith turned to the left of the road and Witty to the right. They left their team, as they did not have time to unhitch it. Evans pursued Witty, and Sontag pursued Smith. Smith looked over his shoulder just as Evans fired at Witty. After Evans fired at Witty, the latter fell and Evans stepped over him with a gun to fire again, though Witty asked him not to shoot again as he was dead already. Smith stopped and fired two shots at Evans, when Sontag stopped and fired at Smith. As he pulled the trigger Smith went down in a crouch and the charge went over him. But Sontag fired again, his shot striking Smith in the back and hands. The charge was a double B shot.

Evans and Sontag now proceed to flee. They threw out their empty shells and reloaded their guns; they then took the officer's wagon and drove off. They were not expected to go far, as one of the horses was stiff.

Joining The Hunt

Detective Will Smith and Deputy Sheriff Witty were shot by the Collins train robbers one mile north of Visalia. Smith was hit in the back, Witty on the side. The wounds are not life-threatening. After the officers saw the robbers getting away, they went back in the house. Smith found in Chris Evans' home the material from which the masks were made, and he was able to confirm the team which the robbers used two nights before was hired in Visalia by John Sontag.

Detective Will Smith is still young and relatively inexperienced, but he had a keen eye for clues and a stubborn determination to catch the robbers. He had been deputized years ago, but just recently moved into a more specialized role of investigator for the Southern Pacific Railroad, and he's hoping to make a name for himself as a lawman. He had tracked down several minor criminals, but this was his first big case. He knew that the Collins train robbery was a notorious crime that had shocked the nation, and he wanted to be the one to bring the culprits to justice. He had studied the reports of the robbery carefully, and he had noticed some details that others had overlooked. He missed his first opportunity at the robbers in Visalia, but he secured evidence of their identity and their escape plan.

Witty was shot under the right shoulder blade and under the left arm. His back and one side of his face were well sprinkled red as he had gone in the poison ivy.

The cavity of his chest was not penetrated, though. Detective Smith's wounds are mere scratches. The opinion was that if Smith had waited for the arrival of Sheriff Cunningham and Detective Thacker, the men would have been arrested.

Evans was well acquainted with the mountains east of there, and the chances were that upon reaching the timber he would continue to evade capture.

Half an hour after Smith and Witty had their encounter with the robbers, one hundred men were in pursuit.

Burke, Pigeon and Pelon arrived at Fresno two weeks after the escape. Pelon and Pigeon made camp and took to rest. They waited for days as Burke left to meet with other lawmen. As they lay around the fire one night, and looking at the stars, Pelon said to the silent Pigeon, "Pigeon, listen here *dear* Pigeon. Have I told you the story of a boy named House Pigeon? House Pigeon, he was much like you. He was strong and curious and wanted to fly like an eagle. So, every day he watched the eagle soar, and he spread his arm while looking at the sky. And every day he thought to hear the eagle invite him to the sky, and he would again spread his arms and look up at the sky and run around like making flight. And he would move around the ground, and think he was traversing the air. And he observed so much. And he practiced so much. Then, eventually, all he would hear is the eagle calling him to flight. Until one day, the boy let go of what was holding him back as he had found that it was himself. He had loved what was around him, what made him the House Pigeon. So, he left the House Pigeon and flew away, far away, high in the sky."

As Pigeon listened to Pelon's story, he felt a warm sensation in his chest. He felt a longing for the sky, a desire to fly like the eagle. He looked at the stars and imagined they were the eyes of the bird, watching him from above. He closed his own eyes and stretched his arms, pretending they were wings. He felt the breeze on his face, he could smell the smoke from the fires below, and the freedom of the air around him. He felt as if he was lifted from the ground, soaring with the eagle, leaving behind the worries and troubles of the world. He felt a peace and joy he had never felt before. For a moment, he was like the House Pigeon, the boy who flew. Pigeon opens his eyes and looks at the sky and smiles. He enjoys these stories.

Pigeon nodded and smiled at Pelon's story. He felt a connection with the boy who flew and wondered what it will be like the next time he sees an eagle. He would listen to the eagle when it spoke to him. As they lay around the fire, telling stories and jokes, they heard a loud hoot from a nearby tree. They looked up and saw a large owl perched on a branch, staring at them with its yellow eyes. Pelon raised his hand and greeted the owl.

"Grandfather Owl, we are honored by your presence," he said. "We thank you for watching over us and sharing your wisdom. Tell us, what do you see in the night?"

The owl hooted again, and then flew away into the darkness. Pelon turned to Pigeon and said:

"Grandfather Owl sees everything, *my* Pigeon. He knows the past and the future, and he warns us of danger and opportunity. He says tonight we rest well, for tomorrow will be a hard ride."

Pigeon looked at Pelon and nodded. He felt the courage brought forth by the Spirit's message and his own determination. He was ready to join the hunt.

The next morning, Pigeon woke up to the sound of hooves and saw Burke riding back to the camp. He had a serious expression on his face and a map in his hand. He dismounted and greeted Pigeon and Pelon, who was heating water for coffee.

"Boys, I have some news for you," he said. "The detectives have convened from Fresno, and they told me that the outlaws we're after are hiding in a place called Sampson Flats. It's a remote area in the mountains, and we need to find them."

He unfolded the map and pointed to a spot on it. "This is where they are, according to our best information. It's not easy to get there, but we have a plan. We're going to join Will Smith's posse. He doesn't know the area well, but he has a few local men with him. We're going to meet them at this junction here and then ride together to Sampson Flats. Once there, Pelon, you will find the men."

Pigeon and Pelon nodded without hesitation. They had come this far, and they were not going to back down now. Pigeon felt a surge of excitement and fear. He wondered if he would finally face the outlaws. He hoped to have the courage when the time came. Pigeon packed his belongings and saddled his horse. He was ready to go.

Having heard of the robber's whereabouts, Burke, Pigeon and Pelon joined Will Smith and a posse of five more men. Pelon was a respected scout and led the group once on the trail. According to the map, Sampson Flats is a remote area in the Sierra Nevada Mountains, about 100 miles northeast of Fresno, California. It is near the border of Fresno and Tulare counties. It is a rugged and wooded region, with few roads and settlements. It is a place where outlaws could easily hide from the law.

Frank Burke

Frank Burke, the deputy sheriff of Yuma, Arizona, was a young lawman of the Old West.

Burke was not a superstitious man, but he had a recurring nightmare that haunted him for years. In his dream, he was riding alone in a desolate landscape, pursued by a dark figure on horseback. The figure wore a black hat and covered his face and carried a rifle that he aimed at Burke. Burke tried to escape, but the figure always caught up with him and fired. Burke remembered the empty and dreadful sight of the horseman's eyes and feeling a bullet hit his chest, and then he'd wake up in a cold sweat.

He never knew who the figure was, or why he wanted to kill him. He wondered if it was someone from his past, someone he had crossed or wronged. He wondered if it was a symbol of his own guilt or fear. He wondered if it was a foresight of his future. He tried to dismiss the dream as a meaningless nightmare, but it always came back to him.

He had the dream again the night before he joined the posse that chased Evans and Sontag, the Collins train robbers. He told Zoila about a singular premonition of the death he was to meet, and she urged him not to go. She said it was a bad omen, a sign that something terrible would happen. She said he had done enough for the law, and it was time to settle down and enjoy life with his family. She said he had nothing to prove, and nothing to gain.

Burke kissed her and told her not to worry. He had been out there three or four times after the nightmares began, but nothing had happened to disturb his equanimity. He said he had a duty to do, and he could not turn his back on it. He said he had a feeling that this would be his last job, one way or another. Frank wanted to end his criminal chasing career on a high note, by capturing the most wanted men in the West. He said he loved her and his children, and he would be back soon. But he did not disclose his fear completely.

The night he started this trek, his dog was filled with some alarm and barked and howled and even caught him by the pants in its efforts to prevent his going. It was unusual for Bones, his dog, to behave in this manner. He left the house, and Bones followed him. The dog was a loyal companion. It had been with him since it was a pup. Bones sensed something was wrong, and he continued to bark and howl and tug at his clothes. Bones tried to stop him from leaving, but Burke pushed him away. He mounted his horse and rode on, leaving the dog behind.

At Howells'

Howells was alerted by his dogs that someone was approaching. He then heard wheels and hoofs approaching his home. Howells got up and grabbed his shotgun, as he was not expecting visitors. He looked out the window and saw the wagon and the horses. He recognized them instantly. He put down his gun and went outside to greet them.

"Hello, Chris," he said in a low voice. "What brings you here?"

"Hello, Howells," Evans said. "This here's my partner, John. We're just passing through n' figured I'll stop by and see how you doin'."

"Of course, come on in. You must be tired and hungry. I'll fix you something to eat."

Sontag tipped his hat, and Evans followed with, "Much obliged."

Both men nodded and smiled. They didn't say much, but their eyes showed gratitude.

He had not seen Evans for a long time, but he recognized him as soon as they came into view. They were riding the Ellis wagon, a black buggy that the supervisor uses daily. Behind the wagon, their horses and a pair of mules followed obediently. They looked like ordinary travelers, except they rode with their rifles cocked.

They are John Sontag and Chris Evans, the most written about bandits in the West. They had robbed the Collins train and shot up a pair of lawmen. They had eluded capture for weeks, hiding in the mountains and changing their appearance.

These men are the talk of town. In fact, they had a large reward on their heads.

Evans is Howells' brother-in-law by marriage. He had known him since they were young men, working as farmers and lumberjacks. Evans is the violent type; always finding the bad side of someone, particularly those of authority. Howells had seen him turn to crime after he was cheated and harassed by the railroad company. He had sympathized with his cause once, even if he did not approve of his methods.

Howells recalls stories of Evans, who once worked at the Fresno grain depot. His responsibilities included collecting seed from farms using wagons and transporting them back to the depot for shipment by rail. Receiving his orders each morning during line-ups, Evans was no stranger to voicing dissatisfaction — whether it was about the volume of loads, location of pickups, state of his equipment, or issues with his team. He seemed perpetually irritated, much to his colleagues' dismay. However, he carried a sense of pride over the jobs he finished and that would allow for the people around him to overlook his behavior. On one particular summer day, as they prepared for the bustling season ahead, Evans was initially delighted to have a pickup close to Visalia, his hometown. Eagerly anticipating a brief visit home, his mood soured when, at the last minute, his boss changed his assignment, sending him elsewhere. Evans lost his temper in spectacular fashion, lashing out at his boss for perceived injustices and accused him of sending him to do the "shit jobs," culminating in insults aimed at his supervisor's intelligence, even calling him dumber than a deaf mule before he stormed off and abandoned his position.

Howells was a respected member of the Dunlap community, where he owned a small farm and sold his produce at the market. He had a reputation for being honest, hardworking, and generous. He often donated some of his crops to the poor and the church. He was friendly with his neighbors and always willing to lend a hand. He valued his good name and tried to avoid any trouble. He knew that his friendship with the outlaws could ruin his standing, but he felt a sense of loyalty to Evans, who was like family. He only helped them as they were in dire need of shelter and a meal, at least he convinced himself. But deep inside, there was a compelling excitement derived from having participated in this event.

The outlaws put the animals in the barn, where they would be out of sight. Evans filled the trough with hay and made sure there was water for them. Howells led them into his cabin, where his two children were waiting. They were startled and scared to see the outlaws, but they did not show much. They greeted them politely and made them feel welcome. Howells' kids prepared a meal of fried chicken, greens, butter biscuits, and coffee, while Howells talked with the men.

They ate and talked for a while, mostly about trivial things. Howells asked them how they were doing, and they said they were fine. They did not mention their crimes or their pursuers, but they all knew what was on their minds. They asked Howells how things were in Visalia, and he said they were quiet. He did not tell them that the town was full of lawmen and bounty hunters looking for them. He did not want to alarm them or make them feel unwelcome.

Evans asked Howells if he could leave the Ellis wagon at his place and if he could return it next time he was in town. He said they had to go into the mountains, and the buggy would not make it. Howells agreed and said he would take care of it. He knew it was a risky thing to do, but he felt he owed them a favor.

After dinner, they rolled up cigarettes and smoked them on the porch. They looked at the stars and listened to the crickets. They felt relaxed and peaceful, forgetting for a moment their troubles and dangers. They talked about Sontag's hometown in Oklahoma. Sontag said he missed the place, and he hoped to return someday. The pair continued to talk, even as Howells left them alone to attend to the kitchen and his kids, but he could hear them talk and reveal details about their exploits.

Interviews

It was Sunday, September 11, 1892, and the party in pursuit of the outlaws consisted of Deputy Sheriff Witty of Tulare County, Deputy United States Marshal McGinnis, Constable Warren Hill of Sanger, Detective Will Smith of the Southern Pacific Company, myself (Deputy Sheriff Frank Burke of Yuma County), a man named Olson, another man named Wilson, Pelon, and Pigeon. These two are from the Yuma people and came here for the express purpose of trailing Evans and Sontag to their hiding place in the mountain fastnesses.

We received a pony message this evening stating that the robbers were at the house of a man named Howells. His place is in the foothills, not far from Dunlap. Howells is said to be the brother-in-law of Evans, or at least to have a relation of some kind. The posse made their way to Howell's place. We were close to Dunlap, so it took the party a little over an hour to get there. Olson and Wilson, the men familiar with the area, pointed at the house. Pelon looked at Pigeon and signaled with his face and eyes down to the ground. It was a subtle command to stay put. Frank can see horse activity leading out, but he has complete trust in Pelon, so he let him be. The posse made their way to the house and the Yuma stayed behind.

Once at Howells, the dogs barked and made their presence known. Howells came out to greet the group. Detective Smith and Frank dismounted and made their way to the homeowner. The rest of the posse remained mounted and circled the home.

Howells was a thin, wiry man with a graying beard and sunken eyes. He looked nervous and weary as he faced the lawmen who came to his door. He knew who Evans and Sontag were, and he knew they were wanted outlaws. He had agreed to let them stay at his place for a night when they showed up unannounced two days ago. He said they told him they were in trouble and needed a place to hide. He said he did not ask any questions because he knew the character of the men.

Howells said he heard the men laughing and boasting in their room that night. They said they had pulled off a daring heist and made off with a fortune and laughed as they recounted the dynamite blasts. They said they had shot their way out of the ambush and left the lawmen bleeding in the dust. And Evans would add, "I will kill that sumbitch that shot up my house!" They said they were the smartest and bravest outlaws in the West, and no one could catch them. They said they would travel to Mexico, where they would live like kings and enjoy their spoils. Howells said he was shocked and disgusted by their words, but he did not dare to confront them. He said he considers them friends despite their gruesome actions and prayed for their souls, and hoped they would find peace someday.

He said the men were polite and friendly and did not cause any trouble. They helped him with the chores, chopped wood, fetched water, and even played with his children. They seemed to have plenty of money, and offered to pay him for their board, but he refused. He told them he was glad to have some company, as his wife had died a year ago, and he felt lonely.

He said the men mostly acted as if nothing had happened. They ate supper with him and told him they were leaving the next morning. The robbers had a horse and cart, which they took from Supervisor Ellis some days ago. They left those with Howells and told him to return them to Mr. Ellis and to thank him kindly in the name of Evans and Sontag for their use.

Howells said he did not dare to confront them but did alert the authorities after they left. He feared they would kill him or his children or burn his house down. He said he just wanted them to leave and never come back. He waited until they were gone, and then hitched the horses and cart to his wagon and drove to Dunlap. He said he was on his way to return the stolen goods to Mr. Ellis, and to tell the sheriff what he knew.

In his telling of the story, when the posse arrived at his place, he at first was reluctant to see them, but he knew he had to cooperate with their investigation. He mentioned he hoped they would catch the robbers, but he also hoped they would not harm them. He also said he still felt a sort of loyalty to them, and he wished he could help them straight.

The line of inquiry continued, and Howells continued to cooperate. Once Frank had reached his limits of useful inquiry, Detective Smith went over the information again, hoping Howells would recall additional information. Frank looked through the window and Yuma trailers were still out of sight.

Camp Found

Pelon and Pigeon watched the posse ride toward the Howells' house. The woods are thick, so they had to reposition as to improve their line of sight. Once the posse was far enough, Pigeon turned and looked at Pelon and lifted his face as to ask what's going on. Pelon answered, "White men are loud like children" and turned his horse toward the trail. Pelon carefully scanned his surroundings. This land is not familiar to him, but he was not at all worried. He had seen two horse tracks leading out of that path prior to the locals finding the Howells house. He kept this information at breast and proceeded to follow the tracks.

The Yuma followed the wagon trail at a steady pace, keeping their eyes on the two sets of horse tracks that veered off from time to time. The woods were dense, and it was getting dark. They passed a creek, and shortly after, the horses they were trailing moved off the wagon trail to a narrower game trail. The Yuma didn't follow it; they instead looked for higher ground and kept riding at a slow pace. The woods got thicker as the pair went off the trail. Pigeon looked around, and every shadow looked like the giant hairy man of the stories Pelon told. He was spooked and looked around. He heard rustling noises in the bushes and imagined bears or mountain lions lurking behind them. He nervously gripped his rifle and wide-eyed looked at Pelon.

Pigeon shivered as he recalled Pelon's story. Pelon recounted how the hairy men of the woods were taller than any human, with long arms and legs covered in thick fur. They had huge hands and feet, and their faces were like those of bears or wolves. They lived in caves and hollow trees, and hunted deer, elk, and bison with their sharp claws and teeth.

"They were not like us," Pelon said. "They speak in grunts and squeals, not with words. They didn't make tools or trade. They did not have tribes or chiefs. They only care about killing and eating. They did not fear anything, not even the spirits of the mountains."

"Long ago, when our ancestors first came to these lands, they found the hairy men already here. They tried to avoid

them and respected their hunting grounds. But the hairy men were greedy and cruel. They started to attack people, stealing their horses and food, and sometimes taking them as prey. They killed men, women, and children without mercy or reason. They did not care if we fought back or ran away. They only wanted to feed their hunger."

Pigeon felt a cold sweat on his brow. "How did our people stop them?"

Pelon smiled grimly. "They did not just stop them. They killed them. All of them."

He explained how the mountain people united against the hairy men, forming a great alliance of warriors from different tribes. They tracked down the hairy men's lairs, and attacked them with bows and arrows, spears and knives, and fire. They fought them day and night, in the valleys and on the peaks, until none of the hairy men were left alive.

"It was a hard and bloody war," Pelon said. "Many of our people died, and many more were wounded. But they did not give up, for they knew that the hairy men had to be wiped out, or else we would never be safe. They did it for their children, and their children's children. They did it for us."

Pigeon nodded, feeling a mix of awe and fear. "Are you sure they are all gone?"

Pelon nodded. "They are all gone. The spirits of the mountains confirmed it. They told our shamans that the hairy men were a curse, a mistake of nature, and that they had no place in this world. They said that they would never allow them to return, and that we should forget them and live in peace. And so, we did."

Pelon noticed Pigeon was deep in thought. He called his attention and said, "Pigeon, be scared of men with pistols." He then pointed to the sky, which he had been studying all evening. "Look, the moon is rising from the south. It will give us some light soon."

After twenty more minutes of climbing, they reached a ridge that overlooked a small valley. They spotted smoke rising from a fire in the distance. They had found the outlaw camp. The Yuma slowly made their way down to the main wagon trail and retreated.

Having put some distance between the outlaw camp and themselves, they brought their horses to a gallop and quickly got back to the trail that turned to the Howells' home. As they slowed down, Pigeon's horse did his signature blow out. The two Yuma turned to one another and smiled.

They stopped at the turn to the Howells' home and followed the posse trail, which led out back to the wagon trail. They were at the posse camp within twenty minutes.

Preparing for Battle

Pigeon and Pelon decided to camp separately from the posse. Pelon had been chanting under his breath since the turn to Howell's house. Pigeon knew it was time to prepare for battle. They unsettled their horses and let them lose to find food and water for themselves. Pigeon gathered wood and prepared the fire. Pelon took his shirt off and was ready to perform a smoke blessing, a crucial ceremony to purify and protect the warriors. They had with them sacred plants like sage, creosote, and mesquite. They stoked the fire and placed the plants in the flames, creating a thick, fragrant smoke.

They removed their hats and bandanas and stood in the smoke, allowing it to envelop their bodies. They closed their eyes and bowed their heads, while Pelon recited prayers and chants in their language. He asked the Spirit and the ancestors to watch over them and guide them in battle. He asked for strength, courage, and wisdom. He asked for mercy for any lives they would take. He asked for a swift and honorable death.

Pelon swept the smoke toward his face with both hands. The mist curled around his aged lines before rising through his long, braided hair treated with black river sediment until it eventually vanished.

The smoke blessing served to purify their minds, bodies, and spirits, and to drive out any evil spirits and negative energies that might harm them. It also brought good fortune and protection in battle, as they believed the smoke created a shield around them that made them invisible to their enemies. The smoke blessing was often accompanied by the singing of sacred songs and the beating of drums, but Pigeon and Pelon did not have those with them. Instead, they hummed softly and tapped their chests, creating a rhythm that matched their heartbeats.

They felt a sense of calmness and confidence wash over them as they completed the ceremony. Pelon said, "Pigeon, get Frank."

Pigeon obliged.

Frank Burke was with the posse. They set up camp in a clearing off the trail and were having dinner. Detective William Smith sent a pony message to Dalton earlier, with the information they had gathered at the Howells. The pony should be back before midnight, and they were eager to find if there is more information coming from the other lines of inquiry.

Pigeon approached the camp with his usual calm and a casual gait. He spotted Frank Burke sitting by the fire, eating some beans and bread. He walked toward the fire across from Frank and signaled toward Pelon. Frank looked up and nodded. He had wondered about the two Yuma scouts. He was eager to finally get a report from them.

Pigeon gestured to the edge of the clearing, where Pelon was waiting with a small fire. Frank hurried to finish his food and then made his way to Pigeon. Frank followed Pigeon to the other side of the clearing. He saw that Pelon had prepared a small pile of dried herbs and leaves and threw them in the fire. He then pushed the smoke over Frank's head, shoulders, chest, and limbs, moving his hands in circular motions. He muttered some words in Yuma, which Frank only understood some.

Frank felt a warm sensation in his body, as if the smoke was penetrating his skin and bones. He also felt a calmness in his mind, as if the smoke was clearing his thoughts and fears. He closed his eyes and breathed deeply. Pelon finished the smoke blessing and sat next to Frank.

Pelon's eyes gazed into the stars, his voice barely above a whisper, as he recounted the fateful battle against the Maricopa. "It was a day of pride and folly," he said, in his tongue. "Pigeon, tell him." Pigeon began translating. "Our warriors, the finest of the Yuma and Mohave, set out to teach the Pima and Maricopa a lesson. We were 150 strong with an additional 150 of our allies, eager for glory and victory. I joined them as a young warrior, I had much hate for the Maricopa, as they had killed my family in a raid. My heart was filled with anger and revenge."

He paused, collecting his thoughts. "The night before the attack, the spirit sent us a warning, a gentle breeze that carried the whispers of our ancestors. The wind spoke of danger, of ambush and betrayal. But we were deaf to its counsel, our ears plugged with the wax of our own eagerness and hate."

Pelon's voice grew heavy with regret. "We ignored the spirit's warning, and instead, let our own desires guide us. We marched toward the Maricopa village called Secate, unaware of the treachery that awaited us. The trek, it had taken eight days of walking, and it was a hot August 31 when we arrived.

"But we were walking into a trap, unaware of the danger lurking ahead. Only a few of us survived the ambush in that small canyon. Chief Francisco launched our attack that morning. We captured the Maricopa village, burning their structures to the ground. But our triumph was short-lived. Weary and hungry from our 160-mile journey, we made the fatal mistake of lingering in the village to rest and feast on captured food.

"As we indulged, the surviving Maricopa women and children fled to Pima Butte, sending a distress call to nearby Pima villages. The Pima warriors responded swiftly, launching a counterattack. But before they arrived, our allies deserted us, leaving my Yuma warriors vastly outnumbered. The Maricopa and Pima forces, some mounted on horses, surrounded us, and annihilated us. Chief Francisco fell alongside most of our men, our bravery and strength no match for the enemy's superior numbers. It was a clever ambush we walked in, unsuspecting, and were met with a hail of arrows and bullets."

He shook his head, his eyes clouding with memories. "I remember the sound of screams, shots flying by my head, and the scent of fresh blood. We were like rabbits in a snare, caught and helpless. I was among the few captured and taken prisoner, spared because of my youth, by the very people we had sought to defeat."

Pelon's voice cracked with emotion. "My captors asked, 'What's your name boy?'

"'Eh-Pelo,' I responded.

"'El Pelon!' They laughed at the play on words. They shaved my head, a cruel humiliation, and handed me over to the American army who took me to Fort Yuma. I was to spend a year in chains, forced to labor under the scorching sun."

A hint of irony crept into his voice. "It was in that darkness that I found a new name, Pelon, repeated to me by a pair of Mexicans who mocked my shaved head. They meant to remind me of my defeat, but I wear it as a badge of survival. And I swore from then on to take the spirit with greater importance than I take food."

Pelon's gaze returned to the present, his eyes burning with a fierce intensity. "Your father saved me from prison. Yet, I learned the value of caution and the dangers of pride. I learned it the hard way. It also showed me the strength of the human spirit, the ability to endure defeat. And it reminded me to always listen to the whispers of the wind, for it carries the wisdom of our ancestors."

"The same whispers are brought on by this night and we best listen and avoid a terrible end."

Pelon said onto his American friend, "Frank, you are a good friend and a brave man. Tomorrow, you will ride with Pigeon and me. We will follow the trail of the outlaws, but when the time comes, you need to move as we do. Do you understand?"

Frank nodded. Although this is not a completely satisfactory report; he could deduce that the desperadoes are nearby, that Pelon knows exactly where they are, and that they will present a danger. He understood the plan, and he agreed with it. Frank knew that the posse was made up of inexperienced and eager men, who wanted to capture the outlaws for the reward and fame. He also knew that Evans and Sontag were desperate and dangerous, and they would not hesitate to shoot anyone who got in their way. He trusted Pelon and Pigeon more than the rest of the posse, and he was willing to follow their lead.

He said, "I understand, Pelon. Tomorrow, I ride with you."

Pelon said a few words in his language, and Frank was off to sleep with the posse. As Frank made his way back to his camp, he felt a strange mixture of peace and excitement, as he prepared to confront the train robbers.

Pelon Leads

The morning of Monday, September 12, 1892, the posse was up at dawn, and they readied the packing mules to start their trek.

The pony messenger came back last night as expected, but he had no news from the investigators in Fresno. Detective Will Smith was disappointed and frustrated, as he hoped to have additional clues or leads to follow. Frank had a more measured response, as he knew that Pelon had found the outlaw's hiding place, and they were close to catching them. He told Will to be patient and trust the process, as they had a good chance of success. He also reminded him that Pelon and Pigeon were risking their lives to help them, and they should respect their ways.

Before joining the posse, Pelon and Pigeon decided to paint themselves with white ochre, a sacred color that symbolized purity and peace. Pelon carried the paint with him from Yuma. He crushed the ochre into a fine powder and mixed it with water and animal fat, making a thick paste. Then they used their fingers and sticks to apply the paint to their foreheads, arms and chest.

They hoped to appease the spirits of the land and the ancestors. They also wanted to show their courage and dignity as Yuma warriors, as they honor the old ways.

Pelon painted his forehead with a horizontal stripe, representing the horizon where the sun rises and sets. He believed this would give him wisdom and vision, as well as honor the creator of all things. He also painted his chest with the image of a coyote, his animal spirit, who gave him cunning and perseverance. He added some zigzag lines on his arms, signifying lightning and power.

Pigeon painted his forehead with a vertical stripe, representing the connection between the earth and the sky. He hoped this would give him balance and harmony, as well as respect for the forces of nature. Pigeon gave deep thought to his chest as he is supposed to depict his animal spirit. He remembers the story of the boy named Home Pigeon. Pelon had told him that story long ago, but he still feels like Home Pigeon, and he's attracted to the eagle in flight. He painted his chest with the image of an eagle, it is the animal spirit which gave him strength and freedom. He added some chevron lines on his arms, signifying mountains and protection.

Pelon looked at Pigeon's paint with satisfaction and put his right hand on Pigeon's left shoulder. He said in his language, "Pigeon, you make a formidable warrior."

Pigeon asked if the paint would help them in battle.

"Yes... It will keep the mosquito away."

They both chuckled and continued their preparation.

The posse was in full force, and they made their way. Pelon and Pigeon led the pack as they headed toward the outlaws' location.

Pelon and Pigeon knew the way to the robber's camp, as they had scouted it the night before. They followed the wagon trail for about 15 leagues, and it led them to a creek. After the creek, Pelon was able to see the animal trail that veered up the mountain. Pelon saw fresh tracks heading out. But it was his intention to provide safe passage to the campsite so that the investigators could look around. He signaled to the rest of the posse to stop. He then gestured to Pigeon to follow him and they took the game trail.

The posse watched them disappear and then settled down to wait. They spoke in low voices, sharing stories and jokes, or speculating about the outlaws. Some of them admired the skill and bravery of the Yumas, who had joined them in their pursuit. Others were wary of them, thinking they might turn against them at any moment. They all wondered what Pelon and Pigeon would find at the camp, and whether they would have a chance to capture the notorious bandits and keep the bounty for themselves.

The two locals, Olson and Wilson, led with this idea. "If those dam' ingin's capture the men, they won't for sure be up to sharing the bounty!" said Wilson.

"They haven't done shit either, we's the ones took 'em to Howells'. Shi-eet, I knowed things turn to shit with ingins around!" said Olson.

Pelon and Pigeon moved cautiously through the woods, keeping their eyes and ears open for any signs of trouble. Pelon knew the tracks could be a rouse and that the outlaws could be anywhere, hiding behind rocks or trees, ready to ambush them. They also knew they had to be careful not to alert them with their own presence, as they wanted to surprise them at their camp.

The Yuma felt safer as they increase the distance from the rest of the posse. They can be stealthier on their own. At about half a league, they dismounted and hid the horses. Pelon was an expert tracker, and he used his senses to read the signs of nature. He looked up at the sky, noting the direction and speed of the wind. He knew that the wind could carry his scent to the outlaws or blow away theirs, making it harder to locate them. He adjusted his course, accordingly, trying to stay downwind of them. He also watched the birds in the sky, looking for any unusual patterns of flight. He knew the difference between a casual bird flight, a mating ritual, a frantic predator chase, and a frightened alarm call. He knew that the birds could warn him of danger or reveal the location of his enemies. He listened to their songs and cries, trying to decipher their messages.

They kept moving forward and Pelon looked around, listening to the critter conversations. He knew that the animals in the woods had their own language, and that they communicated with each other about what they saw and heard. He paid attention to the squirrels, the rabbits, the deer, and the coyotes, looking for any signs of agitation or curiosity. He knew that the animals could sense things that he could not, and that they could be allies or foes, depending on the situation. He used his nose to smell around, looking for hidden stuff. He knew that the outlaws could have left traces of their passage, such as smoke, blood, or food. He sniffed the air, trying to pick up their scent.

Pigeon followed Pelon closely, trusting his judgment and skills. He was not as experienced as Pelon, but he had learned a lot from him. He admired his friend's ability to blend in with the environment, and to use it to his advantage. He tried to do the same, mimicking his movements and gestures. He also kept his rifle ready, knowing that they could encounter the outlaws at any moment.

The two men continued their stealthy approach, getting closer and closer to the outlaw camp. Pelon did not intend on engaging the outlaws, but to gain knowledge of their positioning so he may prepare the posse for success. Pelon identifies a clearing ahead and signals Pigeon to an old fallen tree, where Pigeon went and took cover. Pelon started to make his way around the clearing, but there was a disturbance in the air. He signaled Pigeon to stop and then made his way back.

The forest is alerted with birds flying in escape patterns. The quiet is overcome by squeaks, squawks and flapping of wings. As Pelon made his way back to Pigeon, a faint galloping noise was perceivable. Pelon held his Remington rifle close to his chest. For a minute, he expected to hold his bow and arrows, but he had upgraded a few years back. *Yes,* he thought, approving of the change.

He took a few deep breaths to calm his nerves, and a vision came of the bandits escaping. The Coyote Spirit tells him people won't die, just yet.

They turned to see two riders galloping toward them, followed by the rest of the party. They recognized them as Olson and Wilson, two of the most reckless members of the posse. They had grown impatient and decided to go in after the bandits and put themselves ahead of the Yuma trackers.

Pelon stopped his approach and jumped into the bush. He knew the outlaws are on to the ambush and they could hear the riders nearing. The element of surprise was spent. He quickly signaled to Pigeon to follow him, and they made their way back to the horses.

The rest of the posse had no choice but to follow Olson and Wilson, who had already reached the edge of the clearing. Olson and Wilson had narrowed their thinking to just go after the robbers, without regards to the plan. They drew their pistols and charged toward the camp. They hoped to catch the outlaws, and to cash in on the bounty. It was also their intention to do away with the Indians if they were to present resistance.

But when they arrived at the camp, they found it deserted. The outlaws had left, leaving behind food and copies of the latest newspapers. This seemed to confirm what the men had said when they were at Supervisor Ellis' place, that the bandits read the newspapers and kept track of all the efforts to capture them.

Olson and Wilson, with their guns still drawn, guided their horses to circle around the camp, scanning both everywhere and nowhere in a clear display of confusion. After realizing that the robbers had successfully escaped, they shifted their attention to the boxes and bags the thieves had left behind. They emptied everything that was in their way, looking for the stolen loot. Wilson also looked around for disturbed soil. *Maybe they done buried the coin,* he thought. Olson soon joined him. Their eyes down, they kept looking. They expanded their search to the perimeter edges. And there, behind a bush, "Eureka!" shouted Wilson. He got on his knees and started moving soil. Olson did the same and they dug like mad dogs. And soon, real soon, they yelled "SHIT! SHIT!" as they removed feces from their hands using dirt and leaves. Pigeon and Burke enjoyed the comedy, Pelon remained stoic, concentrating his attention on the forest. The locals now resorted to cursing and kicking items around, and the rest of the posse enjoyed the tantrum.

One voice said, "Yup, you struck gold, all-right." The laughter got noticeably louder.

Pelon gave the investigators more time to take notes of the items left behind before signaling Burke to go. Burke and Pigeon made their way toward Pelon, and he began riding up the mountain. The rest of the posse made mount and within a minute all followed the scouts.

The group followed the trailers up the mountain, crossing through brush and no clear path to follow. The group started cutting toward the south side of the mountain. Burke had noticed that Pelon was following a faint trail. Burke counted four horses on the move, he felt proud of himself for a minute.

The camp was near the Dunlap township and contained a large quantity of provisions. For more than a week, Evans and Sontag had been staying in that neighborhood; a thickly wooded, rough country in the mountains, where they could secret themselves to a certain extent. The camp was discovered by Pelon on the same day the posse was at Howells, he was now looking for the tracks the men left as they avoided the posse. Detective Smith and the investigators noted every item they found intending to find the parties who have been supplying Evans and Sontag with supplies, thus enabling them to keep out of sight.

The train robbers had wandered within a radius of a few miles and were repeatedly seen by parties who recognized them. They were seen by some of the Kings River Lumber Company's flume-hands on the morning of September 10th, apparently enjoying a somewhat meager breakfast of fish, which they had caught in Kings River, and were not in the least disturbed at being observed. This was later communicated to the investigators.

Facing the Outlaws

Evans and Sontag were up early that Monday. They smoked their first cigarette with first light and prepared something to eat. Sontag had cut cheese and added bulldog gravy from the night and made a delicious treat. Evans did the same. They even had fancy cubed sugar for their coffee. They had more than they needed for the following month.

Evans is familiar with Sampson Flats, as he had operated a mine in the vicinity, and is well acquainted with the avenues of escape. The robbers had hidden the loot within these mines days after the theft, and they talked about going back to it every day. They won't let each other out of sight either, fearing that the other might run off with the riches. Sleeping is also difficult under these circumstances. They eat, smoke, laugh together, but there is always an ounce of discomfort.

"When you reckon' we head south to Tia Juana? We have all this money, and it's just gonna rot in the mountain. We should head to the coast, away from the trains and the posse, just like we talked about. I tell ya', that'll be an easy ride if we take the coast. If we just buy that light wagon we been talking about, then we's just travelers finding our way south. Or we get a heavier wagon, buy jars of honey and bee's wax and ride the coast as salesmen!

"I know we can put a lick on any posse that comes for us, but I'm tired, Chris. It's gonna get wet and cold pretty soon. What if one of us gets the sick, running around in the middle of winter? You know they ain't stopping with the posse. We had a good run, but I want to spend some of that money before the law catches up. Listen, we'll get lost in Tia Juana. You can buy that cattle farm you've been talking about in El Rosario; I've heard they have the best pasture. You can send for your family after the dust settles. And change your name, you can be Jorge. I'll start calling you Jorge. I'll ready the mules, we can make it to the loot and pick up a wagon at Dunlap in the same day..."

"I love fish. I'm gonna do just fine on the coast. And you know I'm good with Spanish, si, señor, soy John and quiero tortillas! And I don't mind me all that chili. We'll be all right," said Sontag with a smile to a thoughtful Evans.

Evans usually engaged in these conversations but today he is feeling particularly tired and out of words.

"Or we can split the loot," he said, lowering his voice as if approaching with care, "an' each head our own way. After all, they're looking for two fellars, and we can each take on a disguise. You can be a padre. Padre Jorge, I tell ya', you'll make a hella-good Padre Jorge! I'll buy myself a fancy suit and..." He cleared his throat and refined his pronunciation. "...I will, dear sir, go forth and pretend at once that I am a high-falutin East Coast dandy (pretends to grab tobacco from an imaginary cup and snuffs softly in each nostril)," said Sontag, ending with giggles and mimicking drinking tea with his pinky lifted.

"Let's get the mules and fetch the money. I really don't care how we solve this puzzle; I just know I am not bending a knee to no lawmen. Tell you the truth, all I can think about is going back home, with my wife and kids, an-a I know what you mean, its gonna get cold and wet out here not before long. Get the mules an-a we-a head out. I'd like to clean up, I smell like a wild boar. Let's stop at Young's cabin an-a get cleaned up. If we get a move on, we'll-a make it back here before nightfall."

The pair put away food items, readied their horses, and rode into the mountain.

After the posse left the camp, they persisted in their ascent up the mountain, eventually reaching its southern face. Pelon paused briefly and gazed skyward through the canopy, staying alert for any signs from his ancestors. As he looked up into the sky, he noticed the rest of the posse had gathered around and was doing the same. Pigeon and Burke stood aside observing the skywatchers. Pelon then pointed his finger to one side of the canape and everyone turned, wondering what he was pointing at. Pelon then quickly moved to point at the opposite direction, and everyone followed. Pigeon and Burke now cracked a laugh. The posse bewildered, and voices asked, "do you see it?" "I don't see it!" and "what are we looking for?" They continued in confusion and when they turn their attention back to Pelon, he had already started on the trail again.

A few miles ahead, Olson and Wilson were discussing how the scouts could be lost. The pair hadn't seen a trace for over an hour. "Shieet! These injuns-s lost!"

"Feels like we's goin' in circles!" Replied Wilson.

"You reckon we turn a dosey-doe and look for that trail 'gain? Shieet! Them thieves-s gettin' away and here we are fartn'-r-ound, following that dumb injun! Shieet! I'll go talk to Burke. (Snaps his lips and his horse hurries to the front of the posse where Burke is at.) "Hey Burke, Me and Wilson here ain't seen the faintest from the robbers. Ain't we lost? Let's turn back and retrace our steps!"

Burke replied, "We're on the trail all right; it's faint because the heavy leaf carpet, but we're on 'em for sure."

"Hell! You're so sure we're on their tail, well, let's get to them before they get away! Let's go!" Olson yelled with excitement.

Pelon gently pulled on the reins, bringing Ruby to a halt. The rest of the group stopped as he turned back, his eyes scanning the faces for Olson. With a measured voice, Pelon emphasized, "You, complaining man! Your voice is louder than a crying child!" The intensity of his words cut through the air, leaving no doubt that he wanted Olson to hear him clearly. Ruby, sensing the urgency, pawed at the ground impatiently, ready to move at a moment's notice.

After stopping, Risueño let out his famous blow. "Someone shut that damn horse!" yelled Olson, "You 'just mad 'cause you have no idea where you're going!"

"The horses we're following are not in a hurry. They are not escaping; they are out on an errand of sorts. And you are risking giving our position away with your jawin'." Pelon pulled his club and pointed at Olson. "Keep yourself and your friend quiet or I will knock the teeth off your face and make it harder for you to make any more noise."

Olson stared at the shiny side of Pelon's club for a few seconds. He turned his horse and rode toward Wilson, cursing under his breath, "Don't get told by no damn Indian what to do..."

Pelon glanced around and looked up at the sky. The wind shifted direction suddenly, and he thought, *Speak to me*. The breeze carried a faint scent of wood smoke. The group remained motionless, astonished by Pelon, who appeared to be conversing with someone invisible. "What in tarnation?" Wilson muttered under his breath. Pelon was now experiencing a vision, seeing through the eyes of the wise coyote. He witnessed Burke being shot multiple times and falling to his death. Pigeon and Pelon rushed to assist Burke, only to meet the same fate. The vision startled him, and everyone observing his reaction was visibly concerned.

Years after the wise elder asked him the question, the renowned Yuma scout returned with an answer. When asked, "Eh-Pelo, why are you here?" he understood his purpose: to rescue Burke and witness Pigeon's journey into manhood. And he is now traveled back to the time he was before the group of elders, and after responding, they all are satisfied with his answer. Pelon is now welcomed into that special circle.

"We go on foot," Pelon ordered. The men dismounted and gave the horses to Hill and Smith, who remained on their horses. Pelon, Pigeon and Burke led the posse, McGinnis and Witty followed closely. Olson and Wilson were also on foot.

The tracks led to a wagon trail and the posse continued forward on the trail. The trail traveled toward Sampson Flat, about eight miles northwest of Dunlap and about thirty miles from Fresno. The posse was on its way and had got within about two miles of that locality when they stopped at the cabin of a man named Jim Young.

It was about ten in the morning when Pelon first realized they were near the house. Pelon whispered in Pigeon's ear, in their native language, "You are invisible." Pigeon moved one step to the side of the trail and stood still.

Pelon then moved closer to Burke and whispered in his native language, "Come with me." Burke obeyed and soon found himself dashing through the underbrush at an incredible speed. The surroundings blurred, but he could feel Pelon's grip on his arm. Oddly enough, while Burke's legs were sprinting, he didn't seem to have full control over them. *What is happening?* Burke wondered. They came to a halt at a pumpkin patch, where Pelon left Burke briefly, only to return quickly and placed a large pumpkin in Burke's arms.

"Hold on to this one," Pelon instructed before disappearing.

The posse consisting of U.S. Marshall McGinnis, Vick Wilson, L. Olson, Constable Warren Hill, Fred Witty, Deputy Sheriff Frank Burke, and the two Yuma scouts and one or two others, had tracked the robbers from Dunlap to Sampson Flat about forty five miles east of there, in the mountain fastness. The group was going down a narrow trail, which turned in plain view of anyone who might happen to be in the cabin.

As the posse approached the house of Jim Young, the tension was palpable. The late morning sun cast short shadows across the rugged terrain, and the air was crisp with the promise of conflict. Pelon, with his keen Yuma instincts, sensed the danger before anyone else. He whispered to his companions, urging them into position, but the relentless determination of Olson and Wilson pushed them forward, eager to end the pursuit.

At the specified time, the posse made their way up the wagon trail near the home, with the two Yuma scouts slightly ahead. Olson and Wilson made a rush as soon as they spotted the building. Unaware that Evans and Sontag were preparing an ambush inside Young's house, they closed in. They reached a point around thirty yards from the house. The posse was coming down the trail by Young's place, and no sooner got opposite the trail than the door of Young's house was violently thrown open and Evans and Sontag appeared on the sill.

Suddenly, calm turned to chaos. Olson and Wilson, leading the charge, were met with a hail of gunfire from the bandits. Evans and Sontag emerged from the doorway, their cold, calculating eyes scanning the advancing lawmen.

Without warning, they unleashed a deadly volley, striking Olson and Wilson with mortal wounds. Wilson died with his pistol in his hand, but the two other men were killed before they had time to act. The officers reeled in shock, unable to respond. Seizing the advantage, the robbers fired again, bringing down McGinnis, Fred Witty, and killing Warren Hill's horse.

The encounter at Young's house was one of the most intense in county history. Warren Hill, caught off guard while securing his horse, narrowly escaped a buckshot charge that killed his mount and lifted his hat from his head. Witty suffered a neck wound, but McGinnis fell dead beside Hill.

The surprise attack left the posse reeling. Their horses stampeded, and the remaining lawmen scrambled for cover. Evans and Sontag exploited the chaos, escaping through the back door and disappearing into the unknown.

Those who had escaped the first two volleys of the robbers returned the fire. They were at such a disadvantage, however, that they could make no effectual resistance, much less attack the robbers, who could easily put the walls of the house between themselves and the remainder of the posse. Another man fell under the murderous fire of the robbers, and those of the officers who still had a whole skin left sought a place that would protect them from the unerring aim of the desperadoes. The two Yuma trailers, who were walking down the path leading to the house and remained between the bandits and the posse. A very strange feature of the fight is that the trackers seem not to have received any injuries, although they were in the thickest of the battle.

As the shootout erupted, Pelon and Pigeon melted into the dense underbrush, their figures disappearing like shadows swallowed by the night. Their Yuma heritage endowed them with an almost uncanny ability to blend into their surroundings, becoming one with the foliage. The leaves and branches seemed to embrace them, creating a natural camouflage that rendered them invisible to both the posse and the bandits.

Pelon crouched low, his eyes keenly observing every movement, every twitch of the enemy. Beside him, Pigeon remained utterly still, his breathing synchronized with the rhythm of the forest. The cacophony of gunfire and the desperate cries of the wounded filled the air, yet Pelon and Pigeon remained calm, their senses heightened by the adrenaline coursing through their veins.

Through the chaos, Pelon's mind was a fortress of strategic calculations, his thoughts racing yet precise. He communicated with Pigeon through minute gestures, each one a silent command that needed no words. Together, they maneuvered through the underbrush with the grace and stealth of spirits, their presence undetected by those engaged in the deadly confrontation. Pigeon was eager to fight while Pelon's calm reassured him it was not time.

From their vantage point, they could see the panic and disarray among the posse as Evans and Sontag unleashed their fury. The robbers, emboldened by their sudden advantage, failed to notice the pair of vigilant eyes tracking their every move. Pelon and Pigeon were the silent witnesses, the unseen observers, biding their time for the perfect moment to strike or retreat.

Before the officers could regain their composure, the two robbers unleashed a hail of gunfire with shotguns and Winchesters, catching the posse off guard. The sudden attack left the lawmen demoralized and unable to mount an effective defense.

The battle raged on, but Pelon and Pigeon remained ghosts in the bushes, their forms a mere whisper in the wind. Pelon had listened to the voices of the ancestors. "A cornered animal is the most dangerous," he remembered. An additional disad-

vantage was the undisciplined posse; those men were without hope. They knew to sit this fight out and live to fight another day. For now, they were content to watch and wait, invisible sentinels to the unfolding drama.

Those killed were U.S. Marshall McGinnis, Vic Wilson, and L. Olson. Deputy Sheriff Frank Burke was first counted as one of the fallen, but he missed the shootout. Burke came out of the brush and went to Pelon. He handed him the pumpkin and asked what happened. Pigeon, remaining excited, filled him in with details.

The severity of injuries the robbers might have suffered was unclear, though it seems probable they escaped without harm. Unhindered, they mounted their horses and retreated deeper into the mountains, moving northeast. The pursuers were unfamiliar with the robbers, and it appears that the second group made mistakes similar to those of the initial party at Visalia.

Detective Smith told Constable Warren Hill to go to the Sequoia mill of the Kings River Lumber Company office some six miles distant and telephone the news to Fresno. Constable Hill left Smith and the Yuma trailers with the wounded Witty and dead men and proceeded to the mills, which was the nearest telephone office. Hill had to walk the entire distance and finally sent his terrible tale over the wires to Sanger, whence it was telephoned to this city. Evans and Sontag, notorious Collins train robbers, claimed more victims with their deadly accuracy.

Then, at 2:30 p.m., came the shock that threw the town into a fever of excitement. Sheriff Hensley received a telephone message from Constable Warren Hill of Sanger, who was then at Sequoia, to the effect that Evans and Sontag had been overtaken a few hours earlier in the day at the house of a man named Young, in Sampson Flats, and the story was that there had been a pitched battle in which the bandits had killed three men and wounded a fourth. The report came that McGinnis, Olson and Wilson had been killed, and Deputy Witty was wounded in the right side of the neck.

Sheriff Hensley promptly gathers a posse of eight men and headed to Sampson Flat. Sheriff Hensley immediately started to meet Hill and the others at Dunlap. Parties are being formed in all the small towns of the foothills tonight, and a large body of men will in the next few days give the murderers a hard chase. It is not thought that it is possible for the robbers to escape, their camping outfit having been captured, and it being assured that their ammunition is not very plentiful.

Sheriff Hensley, accompanied by Deputies Pickett, McCardle, and Ashman, set out for Sampson Flat at 3:30 p.m. Meanwhile, Deputy Coroner L. O. Stephens and Dr. L. Maupin left to retrieve the bodies of the deceased, with plans to return by 4 p.m. the following day.

The area around Sampson Flat, located about fifty miles southeast of the city deep in the mountains, presents a formidable challenge for the pursuit team. The officers from Visalia are anticipated to join Hensley's posse, but given the treacherous terrain and the bandits' head start, a swift capture seems unlikely. Furthermore, it is widely believed that the bandits will resist arrest, meaning the posse must advance with the utmost caution.

The community was abuzz with excitement and anticipation, particularly with news of the deceased. Many at first could not believe the story, so horrible did it seem, but when it was confirmed by subsequent testimony, most stood against the bloodthirstiness of the robbers. The entire region is on high alert, and there was speculation that any subsequent attempts to capture the robbers alive would be abandoned; the posse would shoot on sight if the bandits are found.

Under-Sheriff Collyer was busy all the afternoon sending telegrams to the sheriffs of adjoining counties. Sheriff Ray of Tulare was notified and would probably take care that the robbers do not get away by the southbound train. The posse in the counties north of this one would take care to head them off in that direction.

On the night of September 13th, Sheriff T.W. Ray of Tulare County was in Sanger. He expressed his belief that the robbers intended to lure all active forces in the area to one location in preparation for a run to the plains. He suspected that the robbers might attempt their escape by descending the lumber flume or using rafts, and that they would likely disrupt communications by cutting telephone wires.

Upon receiving the news via telegram, the Sheriff Ray has been alerted and will immediately head toward the mountains to intercept the robbers from the south. This heinous event has unified the community, who are resolute in their pursuit of the culprits until they are apprehended. The area surrounding Sampson Flat is now vigilant, making any escape by the robbers nearly impossible.

The men who have gone to the mountains after the outlaws are determined men, and they are spurred on by the desire for vengeance upon the murderers of their fellow officers.

Evans and Sontag have mines at Sampson Flat and are thoroughly acquainted with every nook and corner in that locality. Sampson Flat, where the encounter occurred, is a place with a deservedly bad reputation. It is a rendezvous for outlaws of all kinds and particularly cattle thieves. The notorious Pete and Bennett gang of horse thieves made this their headquarters. The bandits are on excellent terms with all the hard characters living there and have received every assistance from them in eluding their pursuers.

The Capture

The day after the officers were killed at Young's place, Evans and Sontag arrived at the camp of a man named Rogers, who kept horses and cattle. This camp was situated about three miles from Young's location. They approached Rogers and requested food. Pretending not to recognize them, he responded that he had nothing prepared but offered to cook something if they were willing to wait. They agreed, and Rogers began preparing dinner and brewing coffee. Evans and Sontag each carried a double-barreled shotgun, two revolvers in their belts, and Sontag also had a sack of cartridges strapped to his back. Neither showed any signs of injury from their encounter with the officers. The camp was almost directly north of Young's cabin, where the incident had occurred.

Rogers served the dinner, placing both plates on the same side of the table and served their coffee. Evans then moved to the opposite side of the table to have a clear view of the surroundings in one direction, while Sontag watched in another for any danger. They ate without any unusual occurrences. Afterward, Evans offered Rogers a $10 gold piece as payment, which Rogers refused, saying it was too much and that they were welcome to the meal for free.

Evans then said, "Maybe you don't know who we are."

Rogers replied that he believed they were strangers.

Evans continued, "Well, I am Evans, and this man is Sontag."

Rogers told them they could take anything they needed from the camp.

Evans responded that they wanted nothing more than the dinner. When leaving, Evans picked up a Winchester rifle found in the camp and noted that it was unloaded. Rogers confirmed this, and when Evans asked if he wanted it, Rogers declined.

Evans replied, "I don't want it, but if it had been loaded, I would request you to walk a few rods away from it while we are leaving. Since it is not loaded, you need not mind," and with that laid the gun down.

After a brief conversation, Evans and Sontag departed the way they came and disappeared into the woods.

Rogers did not suspect anything until the previous Sunday when he heard gunshots in the distance. Upon inquiry, Evans and Sontag claimed they were deer hunting, although Rogers knew they were lying. He suspected they had robbed another train but hoped no one was killed. Although he disapproved of their actions, he understood their reasons, believing they were good men forced into crime by the greed and injustice of the railroad companies.

Warrants were issued for the arrest of certain parties believed to have afforded protection to the robbers, and it is thought that this will have a favorable result. Detective Smith and Constable Hill are set to arrest four men whom they suspect of being Evans and Sontag's accomplices. George Sontag, brother of the outlaw from Fresno, was the first arrested. Judging from the report of the encounter it is evident that the robbers were informed of the nearness of the pursuing posse by some friend or friends and determined to take the aggressive as the best way of disposing of their troublesome pursuers.

However, the arrests resulted in no gains in information pertaining to the bandido's whereabouts. Months after their second escape, they continue to elude the lawmen.

An intimate of Chris Evans told one of the herders on the flume that he had seen Evans a day or two ago and that the outlaw had told him they were going to leave the country in a while, but not before they had had another crack at the Southern Pacific. The same man states that the friends of the robbers were very numerous in that part of the country and that they seemed devoted to them and would supply them with plenty of food and ammunition and conceal them whenever it was necessary.

Pelon, Burke and Pigeon decided to change strategy. They would no longer place trust in the posse. They will track, survey and capture these criminals on their own.

Their persistence led them to a southbound train. That evening, the moon hovered low on the horizon, clinging to its final moments before setting, and casting a dim light over the train as it wound through thick chamisal. In the luxurious first-class carriage, passengers adorned in the elegant attire of the period settled into their comfortable seats, unaware of the impending activity.

Pelon, hidden in the shadows at the rear of the car, clutched his club tightly, eyes trained on his target — Sontag, the notorious train thief. Sontag was almost unrecognizable. Clean-shaven and dressed in a tailored suit with a jaunty hat perched upon his head, he exuded an air of sophistication that belied his criminal past. He had boarded the train with an air of nonchalance, as if daring fate to catch up with him.

Pelon had been hiding in the car for hours, his muscles tense and ready. He would not give Sontag an opportunity to hurt anyone else. Burke and Pigeon were positioned at the Los Angeles Depot station, ready to provide backup when the moment came. The three had meticulously planned this operation, knowing that any misstep could result in Sontag slipping through their fingers once more.

As the train hurtled through the night, its rhythmic clatter providing a steady backdrop, Sontag stood and stretched. He glanced around, not a threat in sight, then made his way toward the lavatory at the end of the car. This was the moment Pelon had been waiting for. Sontag opens the lavatory door, and an unknown force shuts it back. He looked at his hand, thinking it might have slipped. As he carefully reached for the door again, Pelon's club strikes him on the head.

Pelon's white face peeked out of the shadows and dragged the unconscious body, bound by hands and feet, and later waking to the sight of Burke, Pigeon and Pelon.

After they capture Sontag, the team travels to Visalia. Pelon chose the day, judging the stars and the air. Pelon, Pigeon, and Burke prepared for what would be their most daring operation yet — the capture of Evans.

Evans was a man of cunning and willingness to kill, who had eluded capture time and again. However, this time, Pelon had a plan, meticulously devised to exploit Evans' one known

vulnerability — his love for his wife. The trio knew that Evans would occasionally sneak into town to see her, risking everything for a moment of solace in her company. This piece of intelligence was their golden ticket.

The operation began with a covert surveillance of Evans' home in Visalia. Policemen were stationed discreetly around the perimeter, but the prize lay in following Evans' wife, who often outwitted the watchful eyes of the officers to rendezvous with her husband. Pelon, with his seasoned instincts, deduced that tonight would be the night. The moon was hidden behind thick clouds, providing the perfect cover for their operation.

Pelon, Pigeon and Burke blended into the bustling evening crowd. The market was alive with chatter and the scent of freshly baked bread. Mrs. Evans, dressed plainly to avoid attention, slipped through the streets, a basket in hand. She moved with purpose, navigating the familiar lanes that led to the heart of the town.

Unbeknownst to her, Pelon and his team followed at a safe distance, their presence masked by the lively throng of townsfolk. They watched as she entered a small tavern, one known for its dim lighting and private booths. This was the meeting point. Evans was already there, seated in the farthest corner, his face obscured by the brim of his hat.

The trap was set. Pelon signaled to Burke and Pigeon, who took positions at the exits. They had planned every detail, knowing that Evans' capture had to be swift and without collateral damage. Pelon approached the couple's table with a calm demeanor. Evan's eyes locked on his wife.

Pelon moved with the wind, and a draft accompanied his movement. He timed Evan's hand reaching for a glass of beer. Pelon smashed Evans' hand on the table using his club. Evans shouted with pain, but his instincts kicked in, and he reached for his gun with his left hand. Pelon turned his club around and struck him in the throat. Evans was stunned and appeared to be choking.

Burke stepped in and removed Evan's gun and frisked for additional weapons. Mrs. Evans screamed hysterically and begged the men, "Don't kill him!"

Pigeon guarded the exits.

Evans was halfway in the spasms when Burke shackled his hands and feet. Evans looked up, fear and defiance flashing in his eyes. He knew the game was up. Evans turned, only to find Pigeon at the nearest exit, his revolver drawn but aimed low, a sign that he preferred capture over bloodshed. Trapped, Evans snarled, his chest heaving with the realization of his defeat.

"Evans, it's over," Pelon said, his voice a mixture of relief and authority. "There's no way out."

Mrs. Evans, eyes wide with a mix of fear and sorrow, stepped back, giving her husband a final look of resignation. Evans dropped his shoulders, the fight leaving him, as he saw the inevitability of his capture.

As they secured Evans, the townsfolk gathered, whispers of disbelief and relief rippling through the crowd. Pelon, the mastermind behind this meticulous plan, led Pigeon and Burke as they escorted their prisoner out into the night. The tension slowly dissipated as the reality of their success, orchestrated by Pelon's strategic brilliance, settled in.

They traveled to the local station, with Burke ensuring that Evans was placed under heavy guard. The journey to Visalia's holding cells was uneventful, the once-elusive bandit now subdued and silent. Pelon knew their victory was more than just a capture; it was a testament to his perseverance and tactical acumen.

The next morning, the sun rose over Visalia, casting its light on a town that had slept a little easier knowing Evans was no longer a threat. Pelon stood with Pigeon and Burke, his leadership and courage having strengthened their bond. Satisfaction filled Pelon, knowing that justice had been served through his unwavering determination.

In the end, it wasn't just the law that prevailed but the indomitable spirit of Pelon, who refused to let justice slip through his fingers. His story would be told for years to come, a testament to the power of resolve and skill.

Returning to Yuma

The sun had barely begun its ascent, much like the tired faces of the Yuma trackers. Pelon, Pigeon, and Frank left the passenger wagons and made their way to the box cars for their horses. They didn't wait for the yard hand and proceeded to open the wagon door and dragged the wooden boards they use for a ramp. They unloaded their horses. Ruby went first, showing the way to the others. She peeked her head out of the wagon doors. Her ears swiveling, scanning for any danger.

Pelon walked up the ramp and caressed her face. "It's ok, Ruby, let's go home." With Pelon's command, she looked down at her first step, felt solid footing, and easily went down. The others followed. The journey back from California had been long but triumphant, the successful capture of Evans and Sontag casting a warm glow of satisfaction over the trio.

Frank, ever the steadfast companion, turned to Pelon and Pigeon, his eyes reflecting a mixture of weariness and gratitude. "I'll keep in touch," Frank said, his voice carrying the weight of their shared experiences. "We've been through a lot, it's time to get some rest and enjoy our home."

Pelon nodded, extending his hand. They looked at each other, and they had much to talk. They both had Paddy in their thought and in their heart. But they are not ready to talk about him. But in some ways, that moment said it all. "Be well, Frank. We'll be looking forward to seeing you again."

Pigeon smiled, a silent understanding passing between the men. They had shared more than just miles; they had shared a piece of themselves.

With Frank's departure, Pelon and Pigeon prepared their horses for the journey north. Ruby and Risueño now saddled, the men mounted. The bustle of the train station faded behind them as they rode out, the familiar landscape of Yuma welcoming them back. Their path took them across Main Street. The shops and their patrons continue unaware of their fantastic feat of valor. They reached the Colorado, the river's flow steady, a comforting reminder of home.

As they rode, the conversation turned to the future. Pelon spoke first, his voice thoughtful. "Young Pigeon, we have been far too preoccupied by the ways of the white men. This running after bandits and placing value on gold and silver coins is only a temporary distraction. And we can do well, live the life of the city, eat the food, and drink the whiskey. But we will be lost, and time makes it harder to return. We must return now and find ourselves and seek guidance from the spirit."

Pigeon listened, the words echoing deeply within him. "You lost your parents very young, and I can see in your eyes you have not mourned them properly. I know you can see that in me, as well. We have much in common, my Pigeon. Now that you are older and more mature, you are ready for what's next. You must close that circle, and I must do the same."

"You will find that it is not enough to fight for life and the river," Pelon continued. "You will find purpose in finding yourself, Pigeon. The creator taught our ancestors the Karuk, and in the Karuk you will mourn your parents, seek their guidance, and allow them to return to the spirit. You must cleanse your body and mind. And you must learn. And in learning who you are, your ancestors will live forever. Our traditions make us the People, the Quechan. Our traditions must endure."

Pigeon nodded, understanding the gravity of Pelon's words. "I will honor them, Pelon. I will seek the Karuk and find my path."

The journey continued in reflective silence, the bond between the two growing stronger with each step. As they moved past Fort Yuma, the land around them seemed to echo with the wisdom of their ancestors, guiding them toward a future that honors the past.

By the time they reached the northern outskirts of the old fort, the sun was high in the sky, casting meager shadows over the landscape. They paused, looking back at the path they had traveled, and ahead at the journey still to come.

Pelon placed a hand on Pigeon's shoulder. "We have much to do, and many paths to walk. But we will do it together, following the steps of our ancestors before us."

With a final nod of understanding, they continued northward, disappearing into the mesquite. Their future awaited, a tapestry woven with the threads of tradition, spirit, and resolve.

Table of Contents

Dedication 3
Introduction 5
Paddy Meets Pelon 7
The Glanton Gang 12
More About Paddy 18
Spirit Healers 20
Heepah and Schem 27
Black Sediment 31
Sneaking Up 35
There Once Were Giants 41
Becoming an Observer 46
The Great Flood of 1862 50
Covert Copper 54
Dreaming the Prize 62
Thwarted Ambush 66
Pigeon 72
Creation Story 76
Constables 79
Looking for Pelon 84
Pelon is Found 87
Train Robbery 93
The Way of the Bounties 97
Robbers Identified 100
Joining The Hunt 105
Frank Burke 109
At Howells' 111

Interviews	114
Camp Found	117
Preparing for Battle	121
Pelon Leads	126
Facing the Outlaws	133
The Capture	144
Returning to Yuma	151

www.ingramcontent.com/pod-product-compliance
Lightning Source LLC
LaVergne TN
LVHW041224080526
838199LV00083B/2989